MW00804990

New Directions in Islam

Series Editors
Joshua M. Roose
Institute for Religion, Politics and Society
Australian Catholic University
Melbourne, VIC, Australia

Bryan S. Turner
Australian Catholic University and The Graduate Centre
City University of New York
New York, NY, USA

The *New Directions in Islam* series will promote creative ways of conceptualizing the practice of Islam in new, challenging contexts and present innovative and provocative interdisciplinary studies examining intellectual, political, legal, economic, and demographic trajectories within Islam.

Although recognised as the world's fastest growing religion, many Muslims now live in secular societies where Islam is a minority religion and where there is considerable social conflict between Muslim communities and the wider society. Therefore it is vital to engage with the multitude of ways by which Muslims are adapting and evolving as social and cultural minorities.

How are they developing their faith in line with local and national customs? How are converts and subsequent generations adapting in these challenging contexts? This series moves beyond dichotomies about radicalism, citizenship, and loyalty evident in the proliferation of descriptive and repetitive studies of Islamophobia and Orientalism, which have become both negative and predictable. Rather, contrary to the perception of Muslims as victims of secular modernity, we are interested in 'success stories' of Muslims adapting in and contributing to society at local, national and even transnational levels, such as the case of Muslim middle classes in Canada, the United States, South Africa, and Argentina.

This series will go beyond the geographic boundaries of the Middle East to examine Islam from a global perspective in vastly different contexts from Brazil to Vietnam and Austria to Papua New Guinea.

More information about this series at
http://www.palgrave.com/gp/series/14746

Mehmet Orhan

Islam and Turks in Belgium

Communities and Associations

Mehmet Orhan
UCLouvain
Louvain-la-Neuve, Belgium

The Baillet Latour Fund financed this research for 27 months during my post-doctoral studies (2015–2018) at the Université catholique de Louvain in Belgium. The French version of this book was published by L'Harmattan in 2018. I translated the manuscript from French to English.

New Directions in Islam
ISBN 978-3-030-34654-6   ISBN 978-3-030-34655-3   (eBook)
https://doi.org/10.1007/978-3-030-34655-3

Cover illustration: Pattern © Melisa Hasan

This Palgrave Pivot imprint is published by the registered company Springer Nature Switzerland AG.
The registered company address is: Gewerbestrasse 11, 6330 Cham, Switzerland

CONTENTS

CHAPTER 1

Introduction

Abstract The introduction explores the scope of the research, ethnographic method, and the concepts of community (*cemaat*) and association (*cemiyet*) within the Islamic and European contexts. The research deals with Turkish Muslim organizations. In Belgium and Europe, these organizations are created as nonprofit associations (*association sans but lucrative*, ASBL; *vereniging zonder winstoogmerk*, VZW). Mosques and prayer houses are integrated into these associations. As these associations and federations are built by religious communities, it is methodologically necessary to study organizational and historical features of Islamic communities in local, trans-regional, and global levels, and then analyze the meanings, motivations, and outcomes of their collective actions.

Keywords Methodology • Muslims • Europe • Community • Association

Islam impacts political, social, and cultural issues in Europe. In Belgium, most Muslims are of migrant backgrounds from Morocco or Turkey. It is difficult to pinpoint the exact date when Turkish immigration began in the country, though the fiftieth anniversary of the first immigration wave was celebrated in 2014. Despite frequent mentions of 1963 and 1964 as the start of this process, some immigrants arrived a few years earlier. This research does not deal with immigration, but rather religion in the Turkish

© The Author(s) 2020   1
M. Orhan, *Islam and Turks in Belgium*, New Directions in Islam,
https://doi.org/10.1007/978-3-030-34655-3_1

community in Belgium. Though religious fact exists sometimes within the context of immigration, it is a different research matter.[1]

Historically, Muslim populations in Europe were not formed exclusively through economic immigration as we know it today. Muslim Berbers and Arabs settled in Europe during the Andalusian conquest from the eighth to the fifteenth centuries. The Ottoman Turks conquered part of the European continent, namely the Balkans up to the surroundings of Vienna. The presence of these two empires was the outcome of Islamic dynasties' territorial conquests. During the twentieth century, Muslim Africans and Maghrebians settled in Europe following French, British, and Dutch colonization. Thus, these contexts of immigration represent a kind of physical conflict. Turkish immigration did not result from a process of confrontation; it was based on an immigration agreement between the Belgian Kingdom and the Turkish Republic signed in 1964.

First-generation immigrants were men from central Anatolia. They were escaping poverty to settle in rich industrial regions that offered the possibility of work in Belgium. These individuals tended to be culturally conservative and religiously pious. Their intentions were primarily economic: paying their debts, buying real estate, and gaining prestige and social status. They hoped to eliminate their Anatolian villages of poverty. Most immigrants realized these desires. Nevertheless, the idea of returning, almost universal in the early days of immigration, rarely manifested in actual migration back to Turkey. The fate of these men and women was influenced by several factors and conditions, rather than the simple desire to return to their homeland. Consequently, most of these immigrants did

---

[1] In the West, Muslim populations, including the Turks, were first studied through the perspective of immigration, with almost no attention paid to religious dynamics. The category of immigrant is nowadays less important than the religious category when studying diasporas in Europe. Immigration has long-term effects, and the religious effect is among the most crucial. Concerning studies on Turkish immigration in Europe, see, among others, Nermin Abadan-Unat, *Turks in Europe. From guest worker to transnational citizen.* New-York and Oxford, Berghahn Books, 2011; Stéphane de Tapia, Paul Dumont, Alain Jund (eds.), *Enjeux de l'immigration turque en Europe*, Paris, L'Harmattan, 1995; Isabelle Rigoni, *Mobilisations et enjeux des migrations de Turquie en Europe de l'Ouest*, Paris, L'Harmattan, 2001. Unlike most scholars, Werner Schiffauer is interested in the religious lives of Turkish immigrant people. Schiffauer Werner, "Migration and Religiousness" in T. Gerholm and Y.G. Lithman (eds.), *The New Islamic Presence in Western Europe*, London and New York, Mansell, 1988, pp. 146–158.

not return to Turkey.[2] This book will examine the interplay between religion and other aspects of immigrants' lives. They founded associations and mosques, and organized cultural and religious activities in Belgium, showing the importance of religion among the Turkish population in the country.[3]

Scope of Research: Questions, Issues, and Contexts

This research specifically examines Islam in the Turkish community in Belgium. This is a vast domain, as the religious field is entangled with the fields of economy, culture, politics, and education. The organizations examined herein are those with primary or secondary religious goals, which overtly engage either in Islamic activities or activities with strong religious overtones. In Belgium, Islamic movements are organized as non-profit associations (*association sans but lucrative*, French abbreviation ASBL; *vereniging zonder winstoogmerk*, Dutch abbreviation VZW; association without lucrative purpose in English). Each mosque has an ASBL or VZW, but every association is not necessarily equipped with a mosque. Thus, this research concerns the associative space that intersects most of the time with religious, social, and cultural space.

The research is inscribed within a temporal framework, as it seeks to study the past, present, and future that characterize every human practice. The notion of future refers not only to the relationship between present and future, which is essential to understanding any action, but at the same time to the projections of individuals in the past toward their futures. For example, the desire to return to Turkey of the immigrant mine workers[4] who settled in Belgium in the 1970s and 1980s represents a relationship to the future in the past. Henceforth, "temporality" will be used to indicate the complex relationship between people and the various times in

---

[2] Belgium has a population of about twelve million. At least 450,000 Turkish-speaking people live in the country.

[3] The quantitative research conducted by Torrekens and Adam confirms this fact. In their sample, they show that 91.5% of Turks define themselves as Muslims, and 78.8% go to the mosque. Corinne Torrekens and Ilke Adam, "Belgo-Marocains, Belgo-Turcs – (auto)portrait de nos concitoyens," Brussels, Fondation Roi Baudouin, 2015, pp. 53–54. www.kbs-frb.be/fr/

[4] For a study of Turkish immigration in the coal industry, see Mazyar Khoojinian, *Les Turcs à la mine. L'immigration turque dans l'industrie charbonnière belge (1956–1970)*, Louvain-la-Neuve, Editions EME, 2018.

which collective actions occur. This concept has been referenced by Sartre as men and women's "real relations to the past, and the future,"[5] and by Bourdieu as "the inexorable passage of time and [....] axiomatic trait of practice."[6] Indeed, time orientates people's behaviors by imposing limitations and resources.[7] It defines the frame and rhythm of Islamic action, interaction, and mobilization.

This study has two aims. First, to assess Turkish Muslim organizations from a historical and geographic perspective in order to understand the implications of their networks and activities. Second, to construct a thesis based on a set of common transversal themes within these organizations.

This field of study seeks to provide balanced analysis among the micro, meso, and macro levels of the following question: Why do (immigrant) men and women engage in religious activities? As the study progresses, similar questions will be asked to understand different interdependent factors, such as: What is the organizational structure of Islamic movements? How are they related to each other and what are the outcomes of collective Islamic actions? As shown later, the reasons, freedoms, and constraints of religious people can be explained only in a complex configuration of interrelated networks.

While the topic and question of this research deal with a plural context, the study itself was conducted in a specific and difficult context. In Belgium, there is a particular relationship between religious organizations and the federal government.[8] The federal government recognized the Muslim faith in 1974. The state adopted a law to nominate imams and has begun recognizing mosques as valid institutions within associations since 2005. The Muslim Executive of Belgium (*Exécutif des musulmans de*

---

[5] Jean Paul Sartre, *Critique de la raison dialectique* (Vol. I), Paris, Gallimard, 1960, p. 63.

[6] Richard Jenkins cites Bourdieu. See Jenkins, *Pierre Bourdieu*, London, Routledge, 1992, p. 69.

[7] For this perspective on temporality, see Pierre Bourdieu, *Esquisse d'une théorie de la pratique; précédé de Trois études d'ethnologie kabyle*, Genève, Droz, 1972, and Jenkins, *Pierre Bourdieu, op.cit.*

[8] Policies toward Muslims in Belgium have not been static. Such policies have evolved over time and are characterized by emergent Muslim claims to public space and reactions by Muslim organizations to Walloon and Flemish policies. For more information about these dynamics, refer to Ayhan Kaya, *Islam, Migration and Integration. The Age of Securitization*, London, Palgrave Macmillan, 2009, pp. 93–115; Ayhan Kaya and Ferhat Kentel, *Belgian-Turks: A bridge or a breach between Turkey and the European Union? Qualitative and quantitative research to improve understanding of the Turkish communities in Belgium*, Brussels, King Baudouin Foundation, 2008.

Belgique, EMB),[9] an institution developed by the government in 1994, plays an intermediary role in this process of recognition. Indeed, the federal government acknowledges and pays imams upon the proposition of the Executive, which prepares a file of recognition including information on the status of the ASBL, the record of worshippers (at least 200 worshippers required), a financial assessment, and the assignment of the building as a place of prayer.[10] As such, federal validation of the imam or mosque happens in an interactive context between the Muslim organizations, the EMB, and the Belgian state. This context is extremely fluid, and involves different processes of inclusion, exclusion, conflict, and cooperation which give rise to new issues, like the question of imam training in Belgium.

There are other topical contexts that complicate field work on Islam in Europe. Although this research is not exclusively based on topical issues, these contexts, at times, made it difficult to conduct the research. My field work began in December 2015, just after the November 13 attacks in Paris, and continued through the March 22, 2016 attacks in Brussels. This was also a period where Turkey and the Muslim world went through bloody conflicts such as the Kurdish and Palestinian insurgencies and the civil wars in Syria, Iraq, Afghanistan, and Yemen. Though this study does not concern political radicalism and violence, these events contributed to the subjective experience of the people observed or interviewed, and resulted in anxieties around participants expressing themselves.

Nonetheless, the difficulty of this sort of research does not solely lie in fragile and delicate topical issues. Conducting a field study on Islam or any religion is delicate work. It is challenging to initiate vulnerable and genuine conversation around experiences, thoughts, and religious feelings. Indeed, religion is both a personal and intimate matter and a collective one. All of these factors can affect the quality of results, but the researcher has successfully carried out a consistent study, as the following research methodology shows.

---

[9] The EMB is an official and intermediary institution between the Belgian state and Muslim organizations. It is composed of fifteen elected members. The most important functions of the EMB are the recognition of mosques, albeit the final decision remains in the hands of the federal state, and the designation of Islamic religion teacher in schools. https://www.embnet.be/fr/presentation-de-linstitution
[10] https://www.embnet.be/fr/reconnaissance-des-mosquees-en-region-wallonne. For an article on the EMB, see Caroline Sägesser and Corinne Torrekens, « La représentation de l'islam », *Courrier hebdomadaire du CRISP*, n° 1996–1997, 2008/11, pp. 5–55.

RESEARCH METHODOLOGY

This study combines two methods of qualitative investigation. The principal method consisted of an ethnographic research project consisting of hundreds of hours of interviews and observations which lasted two years, and the secondary method was documentation research.

Archival Research

The documentation research was a study via the Belgian Monitor.[11] This archival research allowed for a global perspective on the geographic situation in Belgium. There are two types of major problems when a study is founded merely on this sort of documentation. The first problem comes from identification: such research does not allow the identification of the association and the mosque according to which ethnic groups or network affiliations they belong to. Islamic terms are commonly used in some organizations, but when these terms are transcribed into Western languages, it is difficult to find the ethnic origins of the founders of the association. Moreover, the terms related to ethnicity and religion sometimes do not appear in the name of the association. For example, the word "Diyanet" is not necessarily included in the name of an association's affiliated with the Diyanet.[12] Then, it is possible to access a large number of associations, but the list would not be complete with only the Belgian Monitor. In order to identify an association or mosque, one usually needs to know the full name of the ASBL, which is the same as saying that a study via the Belgian Monitor should not be the point of departure, because certain information is prerequisite to use it correctly. Finally, there is one last point: every mosque has a number of ASBLs, whereas not every ASBL is affiliated with a mosque. How then can one establish an exhaustive list of mosques? From a general point of view, there is not a single physical or virtual place

---

[11] The Belgian Monitor is an official site that has a data bank of information on nonprofit associations. According to the official definition on the website, "The Belgian Monitor ensures the production and diffusion of a wide range of official publications by traditional (paper) and electronic (internet) channels. The principal official publications are only distributed electronically." https://justice.belgium.be/fr/service_public_federal_justice/organisation/moniteur_belge

[12] The term Diyanet signifies religious practices. The Diyanet is the Presidency of Religious Affairs in Turkey. The Presidency designates imams of the mosques managed by the Diyanet inside and outside Turkey. See Chap. 2 for more information.

to find Muslim organizations. It is thus necessary to use multiple tech-niques of collecting information to assemble correct and more or less complete documentation, which combines the data from the Belgian Monitor with the findings of the field work.

In addition to these difficulties, the most serious problem when researching within the Belgian Monitor results is the fact that one does not obtain sufficient empirical knowledge to construct a text. Even when the researcher obtains a complete list which can enable a sociography of Muslim organizations, it would not be possible to develop an analytical idea, since the nature of the information is not adequate. There is no avail-able historical information. It is not possible to go back a few years earlier, because either this information is not available or the name of the associa-tion has changed. To illustrate this point, one can provide examples. Take the Fedactio (a federation linked with the Gülen Movement),[13] about which the Belgian Monitor offers the name of affiliated associations. But who are the actors who established these organizations? When did they settle in Belgium? Were they born in Belgium? What are the material and symbolic resources of their actions? Another example deals with the BIF (*Fédération islamique de Belgique*, Islamic Federation of Belgium, linked with Milli Görüş, a political and religious movement in Turkey). The researcher made a list of associations via the Belgian Monitor, the website of the BIF, and information gathered from field work. However, it would not be possible to go further than a couple of pages showing the list of associations and some commentaries if the researcher were content with only this sort of information. Such information is then enriched by ethno-graphic research.

Ethnographic Research

The knowledge needed to develop this research was really only accessible via ethnographic work requiring intense contact with people, the research field, and the topic for a relatively long period. Every piece of ethno-graphic research is inherently different, but relies on direct contact with people in a determinate milieu without being distant from them. Distance is an attitude which the researcher should adopt during the analysis pro-cess that concerns objectivity, but in the field, to use an expression by

[13] For this movement, see Chap. 2.

Norbert Elias,[14] the researcher should be committed to gathering information on the reality, thus requiring a long-lasting personal investment, patience, motivation, and work ethic. Indeed, such a commitment enabled me to make participant and non-participant observations; undertake unstructured, semi-structured, and thematic interviews; and engage in individual and group discussions with people who were involved in Turkish Muslim organizations. This component of the research lasted for more than two years. The author observed and talked to hundreds of people of different positions in the organization, generations, genders, and backgrounds (both those who immigrated and those who were born in Europe from immigrant parents). This sampling is quite representative, as it encompasses various categories within the population. The observations took place at mosques, associations, and non-religious locations like the street, cafés, or restaurants in villages or towns within the three federal regions of Belgium: Brussels, Wallonia, and Flanders (principally Brussels, Antwerp and Houthalen, Beringen, Liege, Marchienne-au-Pont, Charleroi, Verviers, and Ghent, all of which are major places of settlement of the Turkish diaspora).

Interviews and discussions were conducted in informal ways. My questions were usually open ended. The interviews were occasionally recorded; more often notes were made, sometimes during the field investigations, but more frequently after having terminated the observations. The proceedings of interviews and observations were not uniform, since they varied given the religious status of the person (for example if the interviewed person was an imam or a practicing Muslim), the age (young or adult), or the movement to which they belong. Questions like "Did you contribute to the foundation of this association?" were used to initiate fluid discussions and enable on-site observations. Additional areas of focus that frequently appeared in these interviews were trans-national factors interacting with local dynamics, and associative activities that depend on Turkish populations in Belgium.

Mixed Methods

These mixed methods developed a body of knowledge which is characterized by at least three aspects. The first aspect is the examination of the interplay between the meso and macro elements at work. At the meso level

---

[14] Norbert Elias, *Engagement et distanciation*, Paris, Fayard, 1993.

is an association, a movement, a district, a village or town, while the macro level corresponds to more global information, namely Islam among the Turks in a larger scale, because religion contains convergent and divergent streams. This allows the investigation of complex movements, processes, and actors. It is an approach that connects ethnography and sociography. The aim was to do a sociography of Islam among the Turkish communities in Belgium, but this sociography was possible, as explained earlier, only due to the accumulation of several ethnographies. This strategy recognizes the value of ethnography, which distinguishes the particular and the general without really opposing them to each other: it implies taking an interest in both the individual and the social.

The second aspect of the investigation focuses on the interaction between historical events, both secular and religious. This research does not adopt a static vision reduced to a timeless snapshot – to use an expression by Anthony Giddens[15] – which idealizes a mode of invariable knowledge dissimulating time and excluding human experience.[16] The research topic is religion in the contemporary period among Turkish communities, while accounting for temporal and historical aspects. This requires an understanding of the way in which Islamic and Turkish norms affect and are affected by historical events. Such observations did indeed enable historical forms of Muslim organizations to be reconstituted. One of the aims of the field work was to encourage people to speak about their own history and the history of their organizations. For example, how did they commit to constructing places of prayer (*ibâdet yerleri*)? When did their movement take the form of an association? I gathered this type of information by talking to people who participated in these historical processes.

The third aspect of the research is the examination of the micro-level daily realities of individuals. To observe the routine, the ethnographer is not necessarily obliged to talk with people, but needs to gain access to their public or private places. This observation occurs in participant or non-participant ways. It gives rises to rich empirical data on religious behavior (for example greeting according to Islamic norms or having a beard) and religious rituals (praying, observing the fast, etc.) Why is it methodologically significant to gather such knowledge? Human beings do not invent new things every day in their daily lives. There is an

---

[15] Anthony Giddens, *Central Problems in Social Theory*, London, Macmillan, 1979, p. 198.
[16] Jean Paul Sartre, *Critique de la raison dialectique* (Vol. I), Paris, Gallimard, 1960, pp. 51 and 53.

ethno-methodological continuity (in Anthony Giddens' sense)[17] which concerns their discourses and practices. This methodological principle is more pertinent in a study of religious fact because the routine, usually linked with Islamic tradition, is one of the bases of power. The ethnographic method enabled the examination of social and historical institutions on the basis of daily observations about the social and cultural practices and religious rituals which are inscribed in these institutions.[18]

Research Ethics on Studying Muslim Communities

Certain research involves ethical questions. In a research project about immigrant, ethnic, and religious communities, every researcher can face methodological and ethical challenges. Opinions in the media and politics on Muslim questions in Europe, far from being neutral, are biased and one-sided. The ethical principle when studying Islam in Europe includes research engagement for scientific reasons and aims. It consists of being objective and neutral in the communication of data through both linguistic and publishing choices to make the information more universally accessible. It is necessary to adopt this ethical principle, which prevents manipulation of the data to serve other objectives than scientific study.

Similarly, the ethical principle relates to questions regarding observation and interviews on religious experience. As suggested earlier, Islam or any religion involves the private and intimate lives of human beings. Obtaining sufficient material to write this book was challenging, because it was necessary to talk to people about their lives and beliefs, or to observe their religious acts. This world is visible, but nonetheless paradoxically closed at the same time. It would be open to research only if the ethnographer holds to certain rules or characteristics. Speaking the language of the interlocutors is an asset, but not a *sine qua non* condition to make people accept being studied. (Researchers can undertake a study on Islam in Belgium while using French or Dutch as well.) Claiming simply that "I am a scholar in the university" does not suffice to convince interviewed people. One should rather construct a real image of the researcher who is neither alienated to them nor dependent on their judgments. Building that image does not consist of playing artificially, but simply requires an

---

[17] Anthony Giddens, *Central problems in social theory*, *op.cit.*, p. 128.
[18] About ethnography of daily life, see Peter R. Grahame, "Ethnography, and the Problematic of the Everyday World," *Human Studies*, Vol. 21, No. 4, 1998, pp. 347–360.

ability to show that there is a rigorous method and ethics of work involved in the collection of information exclusively for scientific ends. Simply put, ethical concerns were addressed through honesty.

Epistemology and Hypotheses of Research

Field research is a source of epistemology and a theoretical framework. Most of the existing epistemology contains unintegrated, neo-orientalist, and Islamophobic thoughts. It does not seem to be founded on a scientifically rigorous approach because of the following reasons. Most of the research on Islam in Europe is not conducted with a precise and clear methodology. The use of methods, the nature of information, and similar reflections about field work are rarely discussed and explored. Media texts and policy-oriented papers generate categories and opinions that are not verified with social science tools. These strategies result in unreliable and manipulative documentation and consequently fail to explain several questions related to religious facts such as mosques, imams, intercultural conflict, the Muslim community, power, and so on.[19] This attitude at the same time is opposed to the axiological neutrality which is essential to social sciences.

The epistemology of this research assumes an empiricism derived from human experience. It is this very perspective that constructs a critical terminology. Religion is examined here via a number of themes and concepts. Some of them, like association, community, mobilization, power, and authority, are more central and deserve clarification, since they are basic to the construction of my research argument.

Although the ethnography generates this epistemology (the link is more detailed in Chap. 3), it was not possible to offer ethnographic descriptions for each argument. Instead, in most parts the reader will find modelization through empirical examples. The analysis of the role of imam, for example, is based on the empirical material, constructed by observations and interviews, but presented as a generalized type, like other

---

[19] There are studies that explore some of these questions, but they remain very few in number. See the works by Stefano Allievi on converted people or the conflict over mosques in Europe. Stefano Allievi, *Les convertis à l'islam: les nouveaux musulmans d'Europe*, Paris, L'Harmattan, 1999, and *Conflicts over Mosques in Europe: Policy Issues and Trends*, London, Alliance Publishing Trust, 2009; or the work by John O'Brien about popular culture of young Muslims in the USA, *Keeping It Halal: The Everyday Lives of Muslim American Teenage Boys*, New Jersey, Princeton University Press, 2017.

figures of authority might be. This text aims to study several micro powers, and so respectful discretion has been exercised toward the personal information of individuals. In general, however, this is a real epistemology which uses the knowledge of common sense, Islamic terms, as well as social science concepts in order to articulate different types of knowledge.

Classical sociology constructed two types of social organization: community and association, *Gemeinschaft* and *Gesellschaft*,[20] or *cemaat* and *cemiyet*. The community is made up of close-knit and relatively inward-oriented relations, emotional ties, social cohesion, powerful solidarities and networks, common tradition, collective memory, and affiliation from birth.[21] The association, on the other hand, is the outcome of industrialization, urbanization, integration with a judicial system, modernism (including individualism), voluntary belonging, mobility, heterogeneity, and division of work.[22] A critical approach to this traditional classification—because more contemporary empirical and theoretical accounts[23] are more complex—will be one wherein emphasis will lie on the hypothesis of interdependence rather than opposition between religious community and association, for two reasons. Firstly, historical classification is derived from an evolutionary theory implying that the association (or civil society) takes the place of community. Despite association resulting from the community, one does not replace the other; they co-exist as distinct types of social organizations.[24] Secondly, it is pertinent, for the sake of nuance, to investigate differentiation rather than opposition. Indeed, there are characteristics specific to each, as membership to an association is voluntary, while belonging to a religious community can depend on voluntary choice and heritage at the same time. Furthermore, an association can share features with a community, like close relationships and emotional ties.

---

[20] The term *Gesellschaft* can designate society or civil society. Here, I use it in the sense of association, which is one of the social and juridical forms of modern society.

[21] Ferdinand Tönnies, *Communauté et société: catégories fondamentales de la sociologie pure*, Paris, PUF, 2010 [1922]. Emile Durkheim, *De la division du travail social*, Paris, PUF, 2007.

[22] Ibid.

[23] See, for example, John J. Macionis, "The search for community in modern society: An interpretation", *Qualitative Sociology*, Volume 1, Issue 2, 1978, pp. 130–143.

[24] It should be additionally noted that even though Tönnies emphasizes the dichotomy, he does not exclude the co-existence of these two types of organization.

Community and association are two social categories which can apply to an ethnic, linguistic, and religious group. Here, I take these two terms in a rather religious sense, which by no means excludes cultural, ethnic, and linguistic aspects. It is rare to find a purely religious community or association, because multiple social and cultural factors (even official factors in the case of an association) contribute to its formation. Nevertheless, it is necessary to underline the religious aspect which a community and association can take because, despite the frequent use of these two terms in several domains, their religious content has not been sufficiently analyzed. A community is religious if the religious links play a key role in its formation and/or persistence. In such a community religion shapes—at least partially—socialization, sociability, identity, or temporality. Individual or communal acts are influenced by or find their legitimacy in religious precepts.

On the other hand, association does not have a sacred feature since it emerges as an obligation of the modern law and system, but our case it is founded by Muslims to organize religion within a legal frame. Indeed, the mosque is a sacred place, especially for prayer, while it has no recognized independent status in Belgium or Europe. The mosque is categorized as a place of worship by law, and it is allowed within a nonprofit organization. Its status is one of "association," which make the study of such associations paramount.

The community alone is not a mode of power; it is this fact which leads us to study the themes of mobilization, collective action, and authority. Islamic mobilizations produce power. Mobilization refers to the process whereby social groups acquire or maintain their material and symbolic resources through collective action.[25] The mobilization herein is motivated by Islamic communities to protect the faith and religious self. This concept is used in a flexible sense, which applies to several collective historical actions such as the construction of mosques and associations. Contrary to what is observed in social movement studies, this phenomenon does not relate much to contestation and demonstration. Muslims in Europe (whether they are Turks or members of other Muslim societies like Moroccans, Algerians, or Somalians) do not take to the street to demonstrate, and because of this fact they differ clearly from workers, left-wing, black, syndicalist, feminist, or nationalist movements. Different from these movements, they build mosques, associations, and schools, eat *halal*, and

---

[25] Charles Tilly, *From Mobilization to Revolution*, Reading, MA: Addison-Wesley, 1978.

pray. For example, there are more than 130 prayer houses or mosques built by the Turks in Belgium. The repertoire of street demonstration is not completely absent, but either it occurs rarely (for example, when wearing an Islamic headscarf is forbidden), or it claims a non-religious cause. For example, popular assemblies for Turkish football or anti-Armenian demonstrations in the street do not identify as religious.[26]

This theoretical and empirical clarification is necessary because many terms in social sciences embrace generalizations, and without precision it would be difficult to understand Muslim institutions accurately.

Mobilization thus consists of activating and reactivating religious practices and representations. Power is closely linked to this sort of collective action by a social and religious movement, and signifies the capacity of a collective subject to constitute itself, and persist. Authority, as used in the following sections, is not synonymous with power, but is a variation of power. Power is a more encompassing phenomenon than authority, so that every social relation involves a relationship of power, but not necessarily a relation of authority. To make these notions clearer, one can use examples in other domains: the father is the figure of paternal authority; the mother is the figure of maternal authority in the family. Both exercise a supreme power over the child, but the child, who has no authority, has a certain power over the parents, since s/he can force the parents to accept his or her demand by crying or leaving home.[27] Another example is developed countries like the USA or others, which hold strong power in the world order, but this power is not exercised necessarily by a single authority: it is exercised by the armed forces, hegemonic culture, or any means of soft power which do not always require direct and brutal intervention to impose themselves in order to be accepted as "legitimate."

This research emphasizes Islamic mobilizations and movements with their varying power and authorities. Indeed, the collective process among Muslims of Turkish origin, embedded within subjective, traditional, and

[26] One of the dynamics of mobilization by Muslim immigrants operates according to the native country. Felice Dassetto, *L'iris et le croissant*, Louvain-la-Neuve, Presses universitaires de Louvain, 2011. However, it is not appropriate to consider every factor coming from the native country as religious. The fact that a person who acts is Muslim and the country of origin is Muslim does not mean necessarily that that action has a religious motive.

[27] Giddens underlines the influence of the child on the parents in order to show power as an assemblage of relations of autonomy and dependence. Giddens distinguishes power and domination, which is an asymmetry of resources. See Giddens, *Central Problems in Social Theory*, pp. 130 and 145.

historical spheres, maintains and generates different forms of authority within communities and associations that are composed of several movements, such as Diyanet, the BIF, the UCCIB (*Union des Centres Culturels Islamiques de Belgique*, the Union of Islamic and cultural centers in Belgium), the tarikat of Nakşibendi (brotherhood or mystical order), the Nurcus, the Alevis, and the Shias. There are three foundations of legitimacy:[28] authority exercised by virtue of tradition, charisma, and legal bureaucracy. There is a complex structure of power, as several titles and positions are structured in dominant and subordinate ways, such as the president of a federation, association, council of administration of the mosque, imam, *vâiz* (preacher), *müezzin* (the one who calls to prayer), teacher, the head of a youth or women's organization, a female or male master of conversation (*sohbet hocası*), and so on. Some of these persons undoubtedly hold more power—like the president of an association or an imam—but in general, the structure of authority is collective. This aspect is evident through the absence of absolute uniformity within each movement, although members of each Muslim group are comparatively more similar to one another than to members of other groups. These movements are made up of different individuals who occupy various positions and roles, which suggests that a dynamic power appears when members and sympathizers are linked by the interdependency of their common works, efforts, causes, and destiny.[29] The structure of authority is hence shared and multifaceted due to the presence of different figures and roles (young, adult, old persons, men or women in each community), and this structure of authority varies given the type of movement (if it is Diyanet, a brotherhood, a Sunni or Shia community, etc.).

Overall, power is not simply constituted by figures and roles. It also depends on traditional, bureaucratic, and charismatic relations which are spatially and temporally situated, and these figures and roles are involved in making these relations. Indeed, human beings cannot develop work, services, cultural activities, respect, brotherhood, or friendship in religious or social senses without assembling, collaborating, or constructing personal relations, or social, affective, imaginary, or bureaucratic ties. In this

---

[28] I here apply the sociology of Weber. See for example *Le savant et le politique*, Paris, Union générale d'éditions, 1963, p. 87.

[29] Kurt Lewin, *Resolving social conflicts. Selected papers on groups dynamics*, Gertrude W. Lewin (ed.). New York, Harper & Row, 1948.

case, this construction is via a combination of near and remote networks.[30] The near signifies relations of proximity between associations and Turkish Muslim communities. Proximity is a way in which Muslim organizations establish religious, social, and cultural ties with the society, depending on various social, political, and spatial dynamics. For example, living in the same district is a territorial condition. Similarly, conversation (*sohbet*), a social form of proximity, constitutes a privileged system of communication. Distance, on the other hand, refers to closeness to social elements from abroad. Relations of Turkish people with their native country, Turkey, seem strong because of politico-bureaucratic, historical, and symbolic (affective) links. As shown later, the Diyanet is linked with the Turkish ministry governed by the government. Milli Görüş gave rise to the associations of the BIF and Saadet Partisi (the Felicity Party). The Nurcus, the Süleymanlıs, as well as the Nakşibendi (Menzil) maintain affective, imaginary, and symbolic relations with the native country.

---

[30] My synthesis of the near and the far is not exactly identical with the Simmelian conception, because the context and the question are here religious. In Simmel, the distance seems to oppose the proximity. This opposition, an undeniable dimension of human relations, depends on the phenomenon in question, as Simmel showed in the analysis of the stranger, who is not an element of the group though s/he is physically situated in proximity to it. In our case, however, a symbolic, sentimental, imaginary, or physical element that is far away is also likely to produce similar effects as proximity does, because what is distant is still a part of the group. Georg Simmel, *Sociologie. Etudes sur les formes de la socialisation*, Paris, PUF, 1999, pp. 599–668.

CHAPTER 2

Religious Movements Among the Turks in Belgium

Abstract This chapter examines Islamic movements and their organizations and activities among Turkish populations in Belgium. The groups being studied are as follows: the Diyanet, Milli Görüş, the Süleymanlıs, the Nurcu Movement, the Gülen Movement, the Menzil Brotherhood, Shiism, and the Alevis. The chapter also includes the Ülkücü Movement, which engages with religious activities, although the movement is not a religious one. The chapter explains how these Islamic organizations mobilize Muslim communities by clarifying their historical trajectories and geographic and temporal variations in Brussels, Wallonia, and Flanders. All these organizations are nonprofit associations. These movements play roles in the organization of prayers and rituals. They also engage in convergent and divergent religious activities such as the founding of mosques, schools, youth and women's education, and the propagation of Islamic mysticism.

Keywords Turks • Islam • Movements • Turkey • Belgium

THE DIYANET

The Diyanet is the largest religious organization among the Turks in Belgium, in terms of both participation and the space it occupies. Its mobilization is concerned with a social and cultural geography which is far vaster than other religious groups. It is necessary to focus on three distinct

© The Author(s) 2020
M. Orhan, *Islam and Turks in Belgium*, New Directions in Islam,
https://doi.org/10.1007/978-3-030-34655-3_2

aspects in order to present and understand the Diyanet: the formation of the Diyanet as a religious authority among the Turks, its organization in Belgium, and the types of religious, social, and cultural activities in which the Diyanet engages.

The Formation of the Diyanet as a Religious Authority Among the Turks

The Diyanet (known also as the Presidency of Religious Affairs or Directorate for Religious Affairs) is a religious institution founded in 1924 in the Republic of Turkey. It was established as a religious and administrative authority during a period when Turkey was increasingly secular,[1] modern, and nationalistic following the dissolution of the Ottoman empire (1922) and abolition of the Muslim caliphate (1924). The roots of this religious authority, however, go back to the Seljuq and Ottoman empires founded by Turkish dynasties. The formation of these states was accompanied by the constitution of the religious authority. The Sheikh al-Islam (*şeyhülislâm*), responsible for issuing religious fatwas (legal advice in the strict sense), constituted the highest religious authority in the Ottoman era.[2] His role was reconsidered once the Ottomans obtained the title of caliphate in 1517, as the sultan had held both temporal and religious power. Sultan Mahmud II established an administrative unit entitled *Evkâf-ı Hümâyun Nezâreti* in 1826 to control the religious foundations (*vakıf* in Turkish or *waqf* in Arabic). Thus, a similar religious authority preexisted, but neither its function nor the context were completely identical. In 1920, the last public institution (*Şeriye ve Evkâf Vekâleti*) to precede the Diyanet was established to carry out the Sheikh al-Islam's functions and manage the affairs of the various religious groups.

The political modernization movement, which occurred after the fall of the Ottoman empire, reduced the sphere of religious authority. The political reforms introduced by Mustafa Kemal Atatürk reorganized religious affairs and leadership structure. The Diyanet was established in this context. It fulfilled two core functions. The first function was strictly linked to

---

[1] Secularism became a constitutional principle in 1937.

[2] There were three types of Ottoman power: *seyfiyye* (military), *kalemiyye* (administrative), and *ilmiyye* (religious). The *ilmiyye* class, whose members studied in *medreses* (religious schools), was in charge of judicial, religious, and academic affairs. The Sheikh al-Islam was part of the *ilmiyye* class.

the secularization of the state.[3] The new Turkish state created a body in charge of religious affairs in order to ensure secularization on the political level. Its second function was to control religion socially, so that the Turkish state could create a homogenous nation.

The 1961 constitution defined the Presidency of Religious Affairs (*Diyanet İşleri Başkanlığı*) as a constitutional institution.[4] A law concerning the Diyanet from 1965 provided a legal definition of this authority: "to exercise the functions concerning the prayers, rituals and morale of Islam, educate the society on the religion as well as manage the prayer sites."[5]

The Presidency of Religious Affairs took on a trans-regional character for the first time through a ministerial commission decree in 1978, when the Diyanet introduced ten posts responsible for religious services.[6] This led to the creation of Diyanet branches outside of Turkey.[7] Today it is present in 113 countries around the world, one of which is Belgium, the focus of this study.

The Organization of the Diyanet in Belgium

The Diyanet in Belgium should not be thought of as a simple extension of the Diyanet in Turkey. Its importance and jurisdiction are not exactly the same: almost all the mosques are under its control in Turkey, while in

---

[3] Rather than arguing that the Diyanet secularized the state, it is more pertinent to discuss why and how the foundation of the Diyanet was part of the vast and complex process of secularization. Indeed, the existence of the Diyanet is sometimes interpreted as a contradictory element to laicism, since it is a state institution that governs religious affairs and provides religious services to society. The way one understands the role of the Diyanet depends on the way one interprets the often paradoxical historical processes. If one considers the Diyanet as an institution created following the abolition of the caliphate, the Sheikh al-Islam (and also as a result of reduction of the role of the *ilmiyye* class), its emergence does coincide with the process of secularization and relating the two appears pertinent. See on the process of secularization among the Turks, Niyazi Berkes, *The Development of Secularism in Turkey*, Montreal, McGill-Queen's University Press, 1964. For a discussion on secularism and Diyanet, see Ali Bardakoğlu, *Religion and Society. New perspectives from Turkey*, Ankara, Diyanet İşleri Başkanlığı, 2009.

[4] https://diyanet.gov.tr/tr/kategori/kurulus-ve-tarihce/28

[5] https://diyanet.gov.tr/tr/kategori/kurulus-ve-tarihce/28

[6] http://www.diyanet.gov.tr/tr/icerik/kurulus-ve-tarihce/8

[7] For an overview of the Diyanet organization in Europe, see Thijl Sunier and Nico Landman, *Transnational Turkish Islam: shifting geographies of religious activism and community building in Turkey and Europe*, Basingstoke, Palgrave Macmillan, 2015.

Belgium only half the Turkish mosques are affiliated with the Diyanet. This difference mainly arises from the fact that the Diyanet is a formal government institution, thus enjoying a special status in Turkey as part of the state. The foundation of the Diyanet in Belgium was in 1982, and approved through a decree issued by the Kingdom of Belgium.[8] Its legal statute is part of the laws relating to international associations and unions which date from 1919 and 1954.[9]

The Diyanet is formally structured as a bureaucratic organization, chaired by Coşkun Beyazgül (a bureaucrat with knowledge of Islamic theology), and divided into several hierarchical units: at the top one can find the general committee, beneath this is the board of directors as well as the board of control. All of these councils are composed of several members or officials. Coşkun Beyazgül served as president of the Muslim Executive of Belgium between 2005 and 2008. He is also spokesperson for the Coordinating Council of Islamic Institutions of Belgium (*Conseil de Coordination des Institutions Islamiques de Belgique*, CIB).[10]

The foundation looks after religious, social, and cultural affairs, particularly among the Turks (Muslims from other countries can also benefit from certain services, especially prayers in the mosques). The Diyanet follows a Hanafi Sunni doctrine and Islamic school of law. It groups no fewer than sixty-seven mosques,[11] and the number of official members is approximately 28,000 people.[12] It comes into contact with at least 5000 young people through religious and vernacular courses organized by associations and mosques.[13] All these services and activities benefit at least 100,000 people. The reader might wonder what this number signifies. Indeed, it would be wrong to talk of a permanent commitment of all these individu-

---

[8] http://www.diyanet.be/Kurumsal/Hakkımızda.aspx. The sources of this information need to be clarified. The site of the Diyanet in Belgium provides useful information; however, the researcher's synthesis on this institution is not based solely on the website analysis, but mostly on observations made between 2015 and 2017 in Belgium.

[9] http://www.diyanet.be/Kurumsal/Hakkımızda.aspx. Even before 1982, there were certain Diyanet missions which temporarily sent imams, especially during the month of Ramadan. Their salary was paid by the people in charge of mosques in Belgium.

[10] According to the EMB website, "the CIB is a civic platform made up of institutions, federations, organizations and dome structures of the Muslim community in Belgium." https://www.embnet.be/fr/conseil-de-coordination-des-institutions-islamiques-de-belgique

[11] Around thirty of these mosques are recognized by the Muslim Executive.

[12] http://www.diyanet.be/Kurumsal/Hakkımızda.aspx

[13] http://www.diyanet.be/Kurumsal/Hakkımızda.aspx

als, even if a portion of them are regularly involved in the organization and work processes. Nonetheless, this vast zone of influence allows the Diyanet to build popular legitimacy.

The map in Fig. 2.1 showcases the geographic distribution of the mosques affiliated with the two major Islamic and Turkish schemes (the Diyanet and the BIF or Islamic Federation of Belgium). Four mosques are affiliated with the Diyanet in Brussels (two in Schaerbeek, one in Molenbeek, and the other in Anderlecht), twenty-two in Wallonia, and close to thirty-five mosques in Flanders.

What are the Diyanet's sources of legitimacy? First, it is a state-owned and constitutional institution in Turkey. In the eyes of the Turkish community, this undoubtedly enhances its credibility. Since the Diyanet is

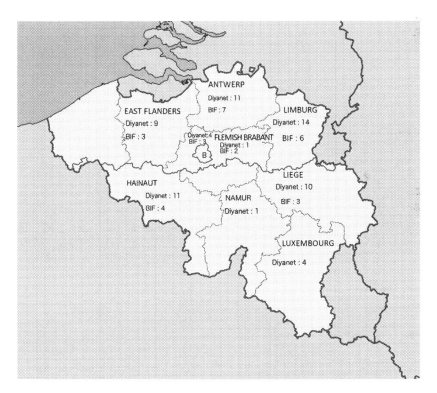

Fig. 2.1 Geographic distribution of mosques affiliated with the Diyanet and the BIF in Belgium

popular and familiar as a state-owned institution, its legitimacy partly corresponds to Niklas Luhmann's concept of the confidence factor.[14] This legitimacy has limits, like every source of authority. In the case of the Diyanet, its source of legitimacy is also sometimes a source of weakness. A religious institution whose legitimacy originates from the state can drive some people to seek an independent source of authority. This may explain why the Diyanet is a major player in the religious field in Turkey and Europe, but its authority is limited, especially since there are numerous other Muslim movements which represent diverse confessional and socio-cultural characteristics, as well as competitions or complementarities between groups.

A second source of legitimacy should be sought within a historical framework. In fact, the Diyanet, which is now a historic institution, went through several stages before it was recognized as a new formal institution during the republican era. Administrative and bureaucratic institutions take time to develop, just as legitimacy and authority do (except charismatic individual authorities). As long as the institutions function, their temporal duration becomes a source of power, legitimacy, and legacy. The legacy of the past is the accumulation of knowledge, the development of a structure which organizes the present and the future. The fact that the Diyanet is a historic institution, especially in the religious field, validates it in people's minds.

The Types of Religious, Social, and Cultural Activities in Which the Diyanet Engages

The Diyanet has a vast repertoire of activities[15] regarding religious, social, and cultural fields. One of its primary functions concerns religious services, which are carried out and organized in the local mosque. I will later detail these religious practices in the mosque, which play a central role in the mobilization of most religious movements. The management of cer-

---

[14] Niklas Luhmann, "Confiance et familiarité. Problèmes et alternatives," *Réseaux*, n° 108, 2001/4, pp. 15–35. For the English version, see "Familiarity, confidence, trust: problems and alternatives," in Diego Gambetta (ed.), *Trust, Making and Breaking cooperative relations*, Oxford, Basil Blackwell, 1988, pp. 94–107.

[15] Activity is understood here in the sense of Max Weber; it is an exterior or private act. Social activity is activity that relates to a collective action. By religious activity, I mean the practice carried out by men and women based on their religious beliefs. Max Weber, *Economie et Société* (Vol. I), Paris, Pocket, 1995 [1971], p. 28.

tain activities and affairs is first and foremost a matter of administrative and bureaucratic management. Indeed, the institution contributes to the construction of mosques, manages them, and designates and pays the salaries of the imams, whose fundamental service is the organization of prayer, one of the duties required to be performed by Muslims five times a day.

A secondary function of the Diyanet is organizing the pilgrimage (*Hac organizasyonu*) to Mecca. According to Muslim belief, each person is obliged to make the pilgrimage once in their lifetime, provided they have the necessary resources. The Diyanet manages trips to Mecca during the festive period of sacrifice (*kurban bayramı* in Turkish; *al-Eid al-Kabír*, also known as *Eid al-Adha* in English, meaning feast of sacrifice). When this is effectuated outside the traditional period of *Hac* (which is pronounced *Hajj* in English), it is called *Umre* (*oumra* in Arabic), of which the Diyanet manages trips from Belgium to Saudi Arabia throughout the year.

Another religious service relates to the death of Muslims. The institution has a fund attributed to funerary charges (*cenaze fonu*) to take care of matters like burial and repatriation to the country of origin; that is, from Belgium to Turkey. To be eligible for this service, each living person pays a premium each year for their eventual death or the eventual death of their family members. In Turkey, this service is rendered free of charge to Muslim citizens; however, since the service depends on transporting the body between two continents, the Diyanet Foundation needs to raise a fund in Belgium.

Religious instruction can be described as a type of religious activity, but is not a religious practice or ritual per se. Its purpose is religious teaching, as well as training of individuals with religious knowledge or religious frameworks. The Diyanet is investing in this field, as it sends religious instructors in coordination with the education attaché to the Turkish Consulate. It has an educational institution called *Houthalen Eğitim Enstititüsü*, the educational institute of Houthalen. It has been managed by the Diyanet since 2013 to form religious staff and employees. The institute is inspired by the *imam hatib lisesi* (Turkish secondary school for becoming an imam) as a reference model. Its teachers are sent by the Diyanet from Turkey. The emergence of this institute can be explained by two factors. Muslim youths are increasingly serving as carriers of two cultures[16] and two languages, whereas their parents only have one culture and

---

[16] For a study about youths, see Ural Manço, "Identifications religieuses et jeunes issus de l'immigration: une recherche menée avec les travailleurs sociaux de Schaerbeek (Bruxelles)," *Forum*, No. 128, 2010, pp. 39–48.

language. As such, they are no longer immigrants, but Belgian Muslims. It is this new cultural situation which compelled the Diyanet to renew and adapt its institutions. Furthermore, the Belgian government increasingly requests that the training of imams be conducted in Europe so that they know the context in its cultural and linguistic dimensions. The institute of Houthalen is an example of how the religious establishment is evolving in accordance with the shifting context.

The scope of the Diyanet is not limited to religion: it also includes social and cultural activities. The latter have two aims. First, they aim to fulfill the socio-cultural requirements of Turkish and Muslim community members, while expanding the Diyanet's sphere of influence within this community. Thus, the Diyanet provides, for example, language courses (Turkish, French, or Flemish),[17] music, art, folklore or theatre courses, and so on. This method aims at a general socialization that is driven by a Muslim religious spirit.[18] Secondly, there are activities aimed at an inter-cultural rapprochement between Muslims and non-Muslims. For example, language lessons in Turkish are available for non-Turks. Similarly, Diyanet associations invite the Belgian people to celebrations during religious feasts, and to festivities of breaking the fast at sunset (*iftar*) during the month of Ramadan.

MİLLİ GÖRÜŞ

The Formation of Milli Görüş as a Religious Movement

Milli Görüş was born in 1969 as a political movement. Its emergence should be understood within the framework of political Islam, which is linked to both Turkish and Islamic contexts in the twentieth century. The Turkish political field went through certain fundamental modifications following the end of the single-party system in 1945–1946. The Democratic Party (*Demokrat Parti*), a conservative liberal party close to the Islamic milieu, came to power in 1950. A military coup d'état terminated the ten-year reign of this party (1950–1960) and culminated in the

---

[17] Turkish-language instruction aims to strengthen commitment to the Turkish identity, although the teaching of French and Flemish languages aims at the integration of Turks into Belgian society.

[18] Felice Dassetto, *L'iris et le croissant*, Louvain-la-Neuve, Presses universitaires de Louvain, 2011, p. 55.

execution of Prime Minister Adnan Menderes. In 1961, a newly written constitution favored the creation of new political parties. This gave rise to new actors who struggled among themselves between secularism and Islamism in the legal political field.

The global context was the Cold War (1947–1991), when the Muslim Brotherhood in Egypt developed as well as *Jamâ'at-i Islâmî* in Pakistan. These movements impacted Islamic thought and action on a global level. It is within this context of plurality of action and ideological emulation displaying the concerns of political Islam that the movement of Milli Görüş was founded by Necmettin Erbakan. Erbakan was born in 1926 in Sinop in the north of Turkey, from a family that was not strictly pious. He studied engineering at the University of Istanbul (graduated in 1948). He went to the University of Aachen to conduct research in 1951, and worked in the factories of the Ruhr region in Germany. In his memoirs, Erbakan argued that several ideologies and parties that governed Turkey between 1946 and 1969 deceived the Turkish people; the birth of Milli Görüş was seen as a response to this disappointment,[19] as the previous political parties failed to develop Islamic projects. *Milli Nizam Partisi* (Party of National Order), the first political party of the Milli Görüş movement, gained representation in the Turkish National Assembly in 1970. The party was dissolved after the coup d'état in 1971. Its followers founded a new party called *Milli Selamet Partisi* (Party of National Salvation) in 1972. The party was part of three coalition governments between 1974 and 1978 at a time when Turkey was suffering from economic crises and political violence between left- and right-wing groups. Although the military coup d'état of 1980 put an end to political parties including *Milli Selamet Partisi*, a new party called *Refah Partisi* (Welfare Party) was founded in 1983.

The Turkish political field of the 1990s was characterized by the success of *Refah* in the local and national elections. The party won municipalities in Ankara and Istanbul in 1994. It won a majority of seats in the national elections in 1995 and established a government of coalition with *Doğru Yol Partisi* (True Path Party, a liberal right-wing party) in 1996. Nonetheless, a "semi-coup d'état"[20] interrupted the coalition in 1997,

---

[19] Hasan Damar, *Avrupa'da Milli Görüş Hareketi* (Vol. I), Istanbul, Gonca Yayınevi, 2013, p. 180.

[20] The events of February 28, 1997 refers to a process launched by a decision of the National Security Council (*Milli Güvenlik Kurulu*) against "reactionarism" (*irtica*). The

and consequently the Turkish Constitutional Court dissolved the Welfare Party in 1998. The followers of Milli Görüş established two political parties: *Fazilet* (Virtue Party, founded in 1997) and *Adalet ve Kalkınma Partisi* (AKP, Justice and Development Party, founded in 2001) characterized by the leadership of Recep Tayyip Erdoğan. The AKP, which has been governing Turkey since 2002, comes from the Milli Görüş movement, but does not define itself as a party of Milli Görüş. On the other hand, *Fazilet Partisi* resulted in a new political party named *Saadet Partisi* (Felicity Party) in 2001, which nowadays defines itself as the unique representative of Milli Görüş in Turkey.

The Organization of Milli Görüş in Belgium

There is an apparent gap between the establishment of the Diyanet in 1924 in Turkey and the beginning of its organization in 1982 in Belgium. This is not the case for Milli Görüş, which launched its organization in 1975 in Brussels, Antwerp, and Zolder. Milli Görüş began to mobilize in 1969 in Germany at the same time as in Turkey. Indeed, members of Milli Görüş, exiled to Europe because of the political conflicts in Turkey, quickly sought to gain a social base within the immigrant community.

Nowadays in Belgium, there are two structures affiliated with Milli Görüş. The first is the Islamic Federation of Belgium (*Fédération Islamique de la Belgique* in French, *Belçika İslam Federasyonu* in Turkish, BIF) and the second is the *Saadet Partisi* (SP). *Saadet Partisi* is a political party founded in 2001 in Turkey.[21] The party opened a local office in Brussels (Schaerbeek) and has about 2000 members in Belgium.[22] Besim Özışık,

---

Council was particularly directed at that time by the military. The process gave rise to the resignation of Prime Minister Necmettin Erbakan (*Refah Partisi*) and to the dissolution of the government coalition composed of the party of Erbakan and the True Path Party (*Doğru Yol Partisi*) in June 1997. The process was characterized by the repression of Islamic organizations and their activities in social, cultural, and educational fields.

[21] Milli Görüş or *Saadet Partisi* should not be thought of as a political party in Belgium or in Europe. *Saadet Partisi* in Belgium operates like an association, its activities similar to other Islamic associations and federations. It plays a more political role when campaigning for the party in Turkey. Political characteristics become clearer regarding Turkish issues during the legislative or local elections in Turkey. Despite this political aspect, its political activities remain less important than its religious activities. Indeed, while there are 2000 members of the Milli Görüş political party in Belgium, its religious movement is, in general, much more significant.

[22] Information obtained in the field work in 2016.

who lives in Verviers, is the party representative. The *Saadet Partisi* also has branches for youth and women. Since the mosques and associations are organized and grouped under the name of the BIF, it is relevant to describe the BIF in a more detailed way.

The BIF, as a federation, is a more complex and larger organization than the *Saadet Partisi*. It is a part of the IGMG (*Islamische Gemeinschaft Milli Görüş*), which can qualify as a confederation in Europe. The IGMG in Europe emerged as a gathering mechanism for various groups of pious workers coming together around small prayer rooms (*mescid* in Turkish) in the 1960s and 1970s.[23] In the 1980s, these groups formed federations that were grouped under the center of the IGMG. This organization is currently present in fourteen countries, including Belgium, with 518 mosques under its control, 17,000 employees, and 27,000 members. It is headquartered in Germany. Its bureaucratic structure is as follows. The presidency bureau (*başkanlık divanı*) is the decision-making organ and the highest body. It is composed of different units: a president, a secretary general, people in charge of the organization, financial affairs, youth, women's section, and *irşad* (this term refers to the concept of showing the just way in Islam). Furthermore, the IGMG is committed to important missions on European and international levels (including Belgium). It has an internal aid association called Hasene International, the headquarters of which is in Cologne. It also publishes a bimonthly review titled *Camia*,[24] which contains spiritual information and covers the events and activities organized by the IGMG, or Muslims in Europe.

The BIF in Belgium has a centralized structure. It is organized as one region and is presided over by Ekrem Şeker (who graduated from an *imam hatib lisesi* in Turkey, and speaks both Flemish and Turkish).[25] Its head-quarters is in Brussels and it mobilizes around mosques. The mosques or local associations constitute small units of organizations essential to the larger body. The federation oversees twenty-eight mosques and associa-tions, as well as two schools. As the map in Fig. 2.1 shows, it manages three mosques in Brussels, ten mosques in Wallonia, and sixteen mosques in Flanders.

---

[23] [Anonymous] *IGMG Tanıtım Katoloğu*, Cologne, IGMG – Islamische Gemeinschaft Milli Görüş, 2014, p. 11.

[24] Its website is https://www.igmg.org/camia/

[25] On the other hand, several national federations affiliated with the IGMG in Europe are structurally separated in different regions (for example, in Germany there are fifteen regions, in France five regions, in the Netherlands two regions, and in Austria three regions).

Types of Religious, Social, and Cultural Actions

Similar to the Diyanet, the Milli Görüş movement combines religious, social, and cultural activities. Its main activities focus on the religious sphere. Milli Görüş is committed to building mosques and nominates imams to the mosques affiliated with the BIF. Based on my observations in the field, I can report that the movement appoints imams who have already lived in Belgium or Europe more than Diyanet does.[26] When the mosque is recognized by the Muslim Executive, the Belgian government pays the imam's salary.

Like the Diyanet, the BIF disposes of funeral funds which function similarly: the fund is in charge of the funeral affairs of those paying contributions to it. Likewise, the federation organizes trips for pilgrimage for those who carry out the rituals of *Hac* or *Umre* in Mecca.

Milli Görüş manages two different types of schools. The first is Virtue, an Islamic school established in Schaerbeek-Brussels in 2015. It is a "confessional teaching school,"[27] which had about 100 pupils in 2015. The second is the Institute of Islamic Sciences Ibn-i Sina, established in Mons near the Belgian-French border. This institute began to function as a boarding school for young women in 1991, and then progressively changed into a school for women, who are residents of Europe and older than sixteen (the two conditions of registration), to receive religious education. The school has about 160 pupils registered. The pupils in this institute all come from Europe and the ban on the headscarf in secondary schools plays a considerable role in student attendance. Moreover, the existence of this school shows the importance attributed to the role of woman within these Islamic structures, because women, as female and maternal authorities, play a role in the transmission of religious tradition and culture to the children in the family.

Lastly, the movement undertakes a set of social and cultural actions which address both Muslims and non-Muslims. The reason Milli Görüş is capable of organizing such a varied repertoire of activities lies in the fact that it is one of the oldest movements organized in Belgium or in the rest of Europe. Mobilization is indeed a question of historicity, which creates

---

[26] In addition, the Diyanet needs more imams, because the number of mosques affiliated with the Diyanet is twice as high as the number of mosques affiliated with Milli Görüş.

[27] *Ecole libre confessionelle* is a specific type of school in the Belgian education system. Its organizing power is a private entity and such schools are generally initiated by religious networks.

a tradition of resources. This is why the movement is able to promote social and community programs like social support to the poor, regular tourist trips in Europe and Turkey, sports and musical activities, conferences and symposiums for students, as well as Arabic, Turkish, French, and Flemish courses.

THE SÜLEYMANLIS

The Süleymanlıs (*Süleymanlılar* in Turkish) is an Islamic community (*cemaat*); its name is attributed to Süleyman Hilmi Tunahan (1888–1959). Its followers call themselves the students of Süleyman Hilmi Tunahan Efendi, or Süleyman Hilmi Tunahan *Efendi'nin talebeleri*. Süleyman Hilmi Tunahan was a *müderris* (instructor in the Islamic school), *dersiâm* (a title given to those who teach during the Ottoman empire, which, like *müderris*, does not exist anymore), and also an imam, scholar, or Muslim master (*maître musulman*). He was born in 1888 in Silistra (in the village of Ferhatlar/Razgrad), which was at that time part of the Ottoman empire, and is currently in Bulgaria. He was trained in Islamic sciences in the *medrese* (Islamic school) to become a *müderris*. Kemalist reforms like the law of *tevhid-i tedrisat* (unification of education) or the closure of *medrese* suppressed Islamic schools and education. The emergence of the Süleymanlıs community resembles the appearance of the Nurcu community: it was a response to the crisis and the emptiness driven by the lack of religious services and teachings. Tunahan served as imam between 1930 and 1936 in the mosque, and was later suspended from exercising this activity, but he was committed to teaching the Koran during the interdiction of religious activities. Similar to the Nurcu Movement, secrecy constituted at that time a mechanism to maintain religious practices. The government officially allowed Koranic courses in 1949 to provide Islamic teaching, which became freer during the period of Democratic Party government of 1950–1960. Thus, Süleyman Hilmi Tunahan founded the Koranic courses. The objective was to train pupils who read the Koran in Arabic script and to diffuse this teaching in society. For the Süleymanlıs, this place and principle of teaching constitute an essential way to propagate Muslim belief.

The Süleymanlıs identify themselves with the *nakşibendi* tradition, and more precisely with the branch derived from İmam-ı Rabbani (1564–1624). This is why the doctrines of İmam-ı Rabbani keep an essential place in their realm, structuring the *tasawwuf* or Muslim mysticism. Süleyman Hilmi Tunahan gave importance to the readings of *Mektubat* (Letters)[28] by İmam-ı Rabbani, which is an intellectual source to the Süleymanlıs. Within the community, people consider that Süleyman Hilmi Tunahan belongs to the filiation (*silsile*) of *Nakşibendi* as the thirty-third chain, and this filiation was closed with him. This aspect is important, because they consider those who direct the community following the death of Tunahan as administrators, who do not have the same grade or status as *nakşibendi* sheikhs. Upon the death of Tunahan in 1959, Kemal Kaçar (1917–2000) and Ahmet Arif Denizolgun (1955–2016) successively occupied the place of leadership. Kaçar was the husband of Tunahan's daughter, while Denizolgun was his grandson. At present, Alihan Kuriş, an architect born in 1979 and a nephew of Denizolgun, is the head of the community. All three personalities grew up within the community and belong to the family of Tunahan. Nonetheless, this is not a religious leadership, but rather it is symbolic. The man who occupies this position of direction is the administrator of the major affairs of the community. He is especially considered as and called an opinion leader (*kanaat önderi*), who helps to ensure the unity of the community (such leadership status is rarely found in Western cultures). This is an example illustrating how the same person can have the status of both a manager and an opinion leader within an Islamic community.

The community of Süleymanlı has had a presence in Belgium since the 1970s. There is no official name like Süleymanlı, neither in Turkey, Belgium, nor anywhere else. In Belgium, the community is officially denominated as the Union of Islamic Cultural Centers in Belgium (*Union des Centres Culturels Islamiques de Belgique, UCCIB; Belçika İslam Kültür Merkezleri Birliği*), which was established in 1979. This means that there was a certain affiliation with the Süleymanlı community within the first generation of Turkish immigrants who founded this association. The UCCIB has been mobilizing since then through cultural and educational centers and mosque networks. Like most of the associations and cultural centers established by Muslims, the UCCIB undertakes religious and cultural activities. It is involved in the religious field thanks to the services of

---

[28] It is a book of three volumes which contains particularly knowledge on *kelâm* (or *kalâm*, the science that studies Islamic doctrines), *fıkıh* (or *fiqh*, namely jurisprudence), and *tasawwuf*. İmam-ı Rabbani Ahmed Faruki Serhendî, *Mektûbat-ı Rabbânî* (3 volumes), Istanbul, Akit, 1998.

the mosque, and the organization of courses on religion within its educational centers. These educational centers enable simultaneously the organization of courses of school support for young Belgian citizens coming from Turkey and the Balkan countries.

The essential content of religious courses consists of the teaching of the Koran. They aim to teach the reading and understanding of the Koran. In these courses, a tiny book by Süleyman Hilmi Tunahan is used. This is one of the few texts written by him and has seven pages. It presents the Arabic alphabet with a didactic technique to make learning relatively quick for beginners who initiate reading of the Koran in Arabic. This book is called a *cüz* (component or part a book), which one can notice any moment when a Süleymanlı milieu is visited.

The color dark blue sometimes characterizes the realm of Süleymanlıs, because in general they wear garments like cap (*takke*), shirt, or pants in this color. I had an opportunity to discuss with one of the followers of the Süleymanlıs the importance and signification of dark blue. It is not a question of the sacredness of the color, but rather a combination of sympathy, symbolism, esthetics, and the historical experience of this community. I was told that the wife of Süleyman Hilmi Tunahan was making dark blue velvet caps when the Turkish state repressed the Süleymanlı Movement during the republican period. It was also a time when followers lived in poverty and gradually rallied around Süleyman Hilmi Tunahan. Since then, they have preferred and admired this color. Dark blue is not the only color the Süleymanlıs wear; they also wear a white cap (*beyaz takke*) and green clothes, as many Muslims do.

Unlike the Diyanet and Milli Görüş, the Süleymanlıs are a decentralized organization. Though I underlined the official existence of this community as the UCCIB federation in Belgium, every cultural, educational center, or mosque established by persons affiliated with the community is not officially attached to the federation. They are administratively independent from the UCCIB. They operate locally and autonomously and not everything is managed by the UCCIB center. The mosque of Selimiye in Saint-Josse, one of the most modern mosques built according to Anatolian and Brussels architecture, is linked with the UCCIB. There are about twenty mosques and associations affiliated with the Süleymanlıs in Belgium, especially in Brussels, Antwerp, Verviers, Ghent, Beringen, and Charleroi.

THE NURCU MOVEMENT

Nurcu is a religious and social movement formed by the followers of Said-i Nursi (1876–1960) in the twentieth century in Turkey. Said-i Nursi, also referred to as Bediüzzaman, was a Muslim thinker (*mütefekkir*), scholar (*âlim*), and man of religious action. He was born in 1876 in the village of Nurs, located in the district of Hizan of Bidlis, a Kurdish province in eastern Anatolia. Two distinguishing factors influenced the life of Said-i Nursi before the emergence of the Nurcu Movement. The first set of factors was political. Bidlis was a place of war between the Ottomans and the Russians in 1878 as well as the during the First World War (1914–1918), which Said-i Nursi participated in and was taken as a prisoner of war by the Russians for two years. He also lived during the period of *meşrutiyet* of the Young Turks (1908–1918), which was a constitutionalist, nationalist, and authoritarian movement. The period of the Young Turks was characterized by the overthrow of the Sultan Abdülhamid regime. Said-i Nursi opposed the massacres of Armenians, since he was against most of the politics of the Young Turks. He witnessed later the dissolution of the Ottoman dynasty, the Muslim caliph, and the emergence of the Turkish Republic, which was on the way to becoming secularized by Kemalist reforms which he did not favor, but rather found preferable to a violent rebellion.

The second set of elements and changes that impacted the life of Said-i Nursi were cultural:[29] it was a time of long and in-depth transformation for the Muslim community, during which changes were implemented in a rapid and authoritarian manner. Indeed, the Muslim societies of the Ottoman empire were going through a crisis because of the weakening of the *medrese* system (namely, Islamic education) and the emergence of new ideological, Westernized, materialist, and nationalist movements, which defined the society and culture outside a religious frame. Kemalist Turkey abolished the *medrese*, promoted the Latin script (which replaced the Arabic alphabet), and invented a new Westernized style of dress. It is in this political and cultural context that Said-i Nursi appeared as a religious leader and the Nurcu emerged as a *müceddidi* movement.

---

[29] The life of Said-i Nursi has been the subject of several studies. See, for example, Şerif Mardin, *Religion and Social Change in Modern Turkey. The case of Bediüzzaman Said Nursi*, Albany, State University of New York Press, 1989.

Said-i Nursi was exiled from eastern Anatolia and moved to Central Anatolia following the Sheikh Said rebellion motivated by Kurdish and Islamic elements, though Said-i Nursi did not defend this rebellion. Indeed, Said-i Nursi constituted a risk for the Kemalist regime due to his charisma and influence on Kurdish society, which would result in a popular mobilization against the government. However, because of his exile, his charisma increasingly extended to the Turkish society in Central Anatolia and resulted in religious mobilization. Said-i Nursi lived for many years in exile and was forcefully displaced between many Anatolian villages and provinces, including Afyon, Emirdağ, Burdur, Eskişehir, Kastamonu, and Barla. He was imprisoned for years and was constrained to house arrest for more than twenty years after his release from prison. This repression did not drive the Nurcu toward illegality or radicalism, but developed a culture of secrecy to maintain their religious activities, which have become much more visible and less secret in contemporary Turkey. Said-i Nursi wrote a great part of his collection of Risâle-i Nur (*Risâle-i Nur külliyatı*) during his years of exile and imprisonment. Not long after his return to southeast Turkey, he died in Urfa in 1960.

The Nurcu Movement, in its own primary definition, is a community founded on the readings and understanding of the books of *Risâle-i Nur*, which aims to do "service" (*hizmet*) in favor of the Islamic religion. After the death of Said-i Nursi, several different Nurcu movements appeared, such as the *Okuyucu*, the *Med-Zehra*, and the *Yazıcı*.

Belgium is a place of mobilization, especially for the *okuyucular*, which is one of these groups. The term *okuyucu* is "reader" in English. It is a religious community which is based on the readings of *Risâle-i Nur* and conversation (*sohbet*). The first circle of *okuyucu* was formed in the 1990s in Belgium; the associations appeared in the early 2000s. There are circles composed of men and the women who gather to undertake these activities in the association. The names of these associations sometimes include the term *medrese*, as is the case for *Risale-i Nur medresesi* in Brussels. In reality, however, this is not a *medrese* in the traditional sense; it functions rather as a house where people enter without shoes, eat, drink tea or coffee before or after conversations, and conduct readings of *Risale-i Nur*. This type of Nurcu house serves as a place of sociability for people in their free time, after school or work. I noticed that both young people and adults, ranging between 15 and 50 years old, participate in the sessions of conversations and readings, festivities with both Turks and Kurds. I observed very close and friendly relations between "members." I use the term in a social sense, because there is no official membership and procedure to enter a Nurcu circle. It depends only on participation in reading and conversation. I remarked that the Nurcu place, as a place of socialization, gives pleasure and contentment to people who gather there. In this space, there is an imbrication of the social and cultural spheres. Religious ties, and society's interest in religion, ultimately develop friendship, similarity, and proximity among people. If not, friendship and brotherhood appear where there is identity, likeness, common values, and interests.[30] These give rise to invisible ties which create the group and the community.[31]

THE GÜLEN MOVEMENT

This movement came out of the Nurcu Movement and emerged during the twentieth century in Turkey. A circle of Nurcu followers, "talebe of Nur,"[32] formed a *cemaat* around imam Fethullah Gülen (born in 1938 in Erzurum, a province in the east of Turkey).[33] Fethullah Gülen served as imam in the mosques of Diyanet in different Turkish provinces, among which Edirne and İzmir constituted two particular places and periods in the formation of the group. The group was committed to undertaking activities in the educational field during the 1970s, which would later become a central space of mobilization in Turkey, Central Asia, Africa, Europe, and the USA. The networks of education developed to be structured around two educational and cultural places during the 1980s and 1990s in Turkey: schools and *dershane*.[34] The educational institutions of this movement are not religious in Turkey or anywhere else, including Belgium. Together with this engagement in the educational field, the movement constructed commercial networks and media channels that also developed throughout the world (in about 160 countries). In Turkey,

---

[30] Tönnies, *Communauté et société: catégories fondamentales de la sociologie pure*, Paris, PUF, 2010.

[31] Ibid. Tönnies makes this point on friendship, but it also seems indispensable to mention brotherhood, which produces informal ties and thus contributes to the formation of religious groups.

[32] The Talebe of Nur are those who read *Risale-i Nur*, a collection of books written by Said-i Nursi.

[33] He grew up in a religious family and his father was an imam. Gülen did not continue his studies after primary school. He followed religious training in the *medreses*, permitting him to become an imam.

[34] *Dershane* is an institution of preparatory classes, formulated for students who are competing for acceptance into high schools and universities in Turkey.

there were about 1000 schools before July 15, 2016, the date of the coup d'état attempt attributed to persons affiliated with the Gülen Movement within the Turkish army. The Turkish government closed the schools and other cultural, media, and commercial institutions. Belgium, like Germany, is one of the European countries which has received many asylum applications from people affiliated with the Gülen Movement since the attempted coup d'état in 2016.

The Organization of the Gülen Movement in Belgium

A particularity of the movement is that it does not mobilize around the mosques, either in Belgium or anywhere else. This strategy is what makes this movement different from most of the other Turkish and Arabic religious organizations (there are mosques established, for example in the UK, but this is rare). This means that the networks operate in a different manner within society and culture, comparatively. The networks of the movement have been present in Belgium since 1988–1989, but became institutionalized around 1997, via the foundation of a cultural association in Brussels. Through the multiplication of associations, the movement subsequently formed a network in civil society inscribed within several social, economic, and cultural dynamics. The majority of these associations are organized within a federation (an umbrella organization according to its own definition) called the FEDACTIO (Federation of Active Associations in Belgium, established in 2010; *Belçika Aktif Dernekler Federasyonu* in Turkish; *Federation des Associations Actives en Belgique* in French; *Federatie van Actieve Vereningingen van Belgie* in Flemish). The BETIAD (Association of Turkish and Belgian Entrepreneurs, founded in 1997; *Association d'entrepreneurs turcs et belges* in French; *Belçika Türk İşadamları Derneği* in Turkish; *Federatie van Actieve Ondernemers van Belgie* in Flemish) is another type of association which gathers industrial entrepreneurs. (According to its website, it assembled nearly 1200 entrepreneurs in 2016.[35]) Similar to the FEDACTIO, of which it is a founding member, the BETIAD operates on a national scale in the following regions: Brussels, Antwerp, Hainaut, Liège, Limburg, and Ghent.

The Gülen Movement in Belgium is not necessarily composed or developed by the generation of immigrant workers who arrived in Belgium in the 1960s and 1970s. Most of the associations have been established by

[35] The website for Betiad is www.betiad.be

young people, as they have cultural experience, knowledge, education, and university diplomas. This structural disposition shapes, in part, the mobilization, as will be presented below.

The network of the Gülen Movement manages two series of schools, which have dozens of entities. The difference between the two linguistic regimes is the schools of Lucerna, taught in Flemish, and *écoles des Etoiles* (schools of stars), which are taught in French. Both types are free non-denominational schools (*écoles libres non confessionnelles*) that offer primary and secondary education. The schools called Lucerna consist of four secondary schools (*collèges*, which are situated in Antwerp, Brussels, Ghent, and Houthalen) and three basis schools (in Hoboken, Anderlecht, and Genk), whereas the *écoles des Etoiles*, the first of which appeared in 2005, are five educational institutions, namely two secondary schools (Brussels and Charleroi) and three primary schools (Brussels, Charleroi, Liège).

The emergence of these schools needs to be studied in more detail (which is beyond the scope of this study), but one can assume a few characteristics of these schools. Their foundation corresponds to a period of development in Islamic networks in Turkey during the 2000s. Two religious movements, the AKP in the political field and the Gülen Movement in the social, economic, and cultural fields, maximized their interests against Kemalist actors in Turkey. It was then a time when power relations changed in favor of Islamic organizations. The extension of the Gülen Movement may have increased its legitimacy and power within the Turkish communities in Belgium. Nonetheless, the impact of social, cultural, and political issues related to Turkey would never be a unique determinant. Indeed, the appearance of the schools is derived from a cultural and educational need within the context of demographic expansion. This argument is based on my general observations and certain texts which cite this factor, although it is unfortunately not possible to establish the statistics to prove it.[36] (The argument also can apply to the schools of the Milli Görüş.) The schools were generally established in urban districts which are ethnically mixed. These schools are typically places that are easy to access for students, who can avoid making long trips during the day. This technical factor, seemingly banal at first sight, becomes important as long as the schools offer a quality education to pupils coming from the families of the

---

[36] See, for example, Pierre Bouillon, "Secondaire: il manque 13 écoles, dont 12 à Bruxelles," *Le Soir* (the blog), 4 May 2012.

middle class, who are motivated by social mobility. The education is not religious, as underlined earlier. The terms *étoile* (meaning star in English) and Lucerna suggest the idea of "something that shines and to which one should get closer," or a "guide that enlightens and orients." These terms do not have a religious connotation, necessarily. Comparatively, they are used less religiously than the term "virtue," which is the name of a school of the Milli Görüş (the BIF), which evokes a moral and conservative notion. More than half of the pupils of the schools, similar to those of the Milli Görüş, come from Muslim families with Turkish and Moroccan origins or from the Balkan countries. Nevertheless, one should specify that neither the pupils nor the instructors come exclusively from the Muslim immigrant population, as there are many non-Muslim students and instructors.

There are two features of the organization of power. The schools are founded by the support of a group of Turkish-Muslim businessmen, parents, and instructors. Once they fulfill a certain number of administrative criteria, especially a sufficient number of students being reached, they are subsidized by the Wallonia or Flemish Federation. These entrepreneurs legitimize the foundation of the schools through moralism and civism in their discourses. The schools' websites refer to similar symbols, as the supporters or followers of the Gülen Movement try to engage frequently in intercultural dialogue. Terms such as moral, civil, or civism have positive connotations, but nevertheless seem too vast. It would be relevant to explain how these actors construct themselves in a general manner and how this self-construction is being confronted with resistance from those who oppose them, either in Turkey or in the rest of the world. The movement has been defining itself as *Hizmet* (service) for several decades, in the sense that a service is rendered to society through education and teaching. The notion of *cemaat* is used together with *Hizmet* for self-definition: while the latter refers to the action, the former refers to the identity of the group. However, both of them have been contested since the 1990s in different ways. Kemalist actors identified the movement as reactionary (*irticacı*), while the AKP began to define it as a structure invading the Turkish state in 2012–2013. In short, the categories which the movement members constructed for themselves enter into conflict with their opponents to define the reality—which is variable given the time—and this symbolic conflict structures the field of power. As the actors and their mutual relations of power evolve, the conflict takes on new characteristics. Why do I mention these internal struggles which Turkey has been going through for years? Indeed, the autonomy of these types of religious groups, in the Belgian context, seems to be limited, given the scope of these conflicts and the number of actors involved. The Gülen Movement's room for maneuver has decreased in Belgium since the conflict began with the Turkish government in 2012. Because support within Turkish society has decreased considerably since July 15, 2016, the possibilities for action remain limited for persons affiliated with the movement.

Types of Activities of the Movement

The typologies of action which I constructed to present to the principal groups are necessary to categorize the activities of the Gülen Movement as well. There are four types of action: commerce, such as the activities of the BETIAD; media; education; and intercultural dialogue. Thus, it is concluded that similar types of activities characterize several religious movements, as one can find similar activities organized by the Diyanet, the BIF, or the Gülen Movement. There are, however, major differences in the Gülen Movement as well, since its activities are not hierarchized in the same manner as other Turkish religious organizations. Indeed, intercultural dialogue constitutes a central mode of action for the movement thanks to the platform of Intercultural Dialogue located in Brussels, which organizes conferences and invites European academics, journalists, or politicians as moderators. In other Islamic groups, there is no specialized section to organize such activities; rather, they are integrated with cultural activities. Furthermore, the media affiliated with Gülen was more influential and organized, until July 2016, while other groups did not have their own media channels in Belgium. (Turkish-speaking people consult the newspapers and watch TV channels transmitted from Turkey, but their cultural, popular, and nationalist aspects are much more important than the religious ones because they are not Islamic media.) Zaman Belgique (Zaman Belgium), a newspaper published exclusively in Belgium and Luxembourg, was closed in August 2016. This is one of the indicators which shows the conflict between the Gülen Movement and the Turkish government, and how these actions subsequently narrowed the field of mobilization while decreasing its agency; namely, the capacity for action in Belgium. Finally, educational institutions affiliated with the movement are more numerous, and there is a chair of Fethullah Gülen specialized in studies of the Gülen Movement at the Katholieke Universiteit te Leuven.

After the failed coup d'état in July 2016 in Turkey, the structure of the movement was substantially weakened, but it persists outside the country. However, the networks of power lost strength in Belgium, as in several countries throughout the world. This weakening depends on multiple factors. The first is linked with effects of the conflict with the AKP government. Popular support for and the social legitimacy of the movement have decreased within Turkish communities in both Turkey and Europe since 2012, in particular after July 15, 2016. Indeed, the confrontation of an Islamic movement with the Turkish government or state is likely to produce negative effects on the public perception of such a movement. These effects were even more negative on the Gülen Movement, because the AKP is a political party coming from an Islamic movement. Second, the repression of the Turkish government led to important cadres in Turkey being jailed, and the defection of some members who ultimately abandoned the cause and the organization. Finally, the financing of the movement weakened after the confiscation of enterprises and the interdiction of educational and commercial activities by the government in Turkey. Consequently, the relation of the movement with the state and society profoundly changed between 2012 and 2018 in Turkey: the movement maintains its activities almost exclusively within the diaspora. One should underline that the politics of Muslim countries' government significantly impacts the public opinion of immigrant societies living in Europe, and this seems not to be limited to Turkish immigrants. I do not have statistical confirmation, but I witnessed evidence that after the closure of the Gülen Movement in Morocco on the demand of the AKP, certain Moroccan families withdrew their children from the *écoles des Etoiles* in Wallonia.

THE NATIONALIST ÜLKÜCÜ MOVEMENT AND RELIGION

The Ülkücü Movement as a Historical Category in the Turkish World

The Ülkücü Movement is a Turkish nationalist movement which began in the 1940s, and was organized for the first time as a political party in the 1960s in Turkey. Influenced by the radical Turkist ideas of Nihal Atsız (1905–1975), the movement grew under the leadership of Colonel Alparslan Türkeş (1917–1997). Indeed, the arrest of these two personalities gave rise to the formation of a Turkist protest group in Ankara in

1944. The passage to a multi-party system in 1945, and the establishment of a new liberal constitution in 1961, favored the emergence of new political parties in the Turkish political system. Thus, *Cumhuriyetçi Köylü Millet Partisi* (Republican Peasants' Nation Party) was founded in 1958 as the first political party representing the Ülkücü Movement. The party took the name of *Milliyetçi Hareket Partisi* (MHP – Nationalist Action Party) in 1969, and the MHP was dissolved after the military coup d'état in 1980. The group was then reestablished in 1993. Today, it is the fourth largest party in the Turkish National Assembly.

The MHP never gained power by becoming the party with the most seats in legislative elections. Nonetheless, it generally won an average of 10 percent of the votes within the National Assembly, varying given the historical conjunctures. The party sometimes directed government coalitions, for example between 1999 and 2002. The MHP should be considered both a political party and a social movement. Indeed, it is a right-wing political party which has organized social movements and demonstrations in the street, which at times have resulted in acts of political violence. This habitus of the movement is derived from the cleavages that occurred between the radical left- and right-wing groups during the 1960s and 1970s, and has been recurring since then, depending on the Kurdish conflict in question.

The word *ülkücü* can literally be translated as "idealists," the term which I use to refer to those who belong to this movement. The English texts sometimes refer to Ülkücü as Grey Wolves (*bozkurtlar* in Turkish), a term employed by Türkeş to designate the Ülkücü youth, which was later more frequently used.[37] The symbolic field of the movement is represented by three moon crescents and a wolf howling in front of a red background. The animal is shaped by a hand that forms the head of the wolf by keeping the index finger and little finger straight, and then curling the middle and ring fingers to touch the thumb. The wolf is a political sign which one can notice among Ülkücü members in Turkey and Europe, including Belgium. In general, Islamic movements do not employ this type of sign and totemic symbol to represent themselves. It is one of the features specific to cultural, ethnic, and nationalist groups, showing that this movement is essentially nationalist.

---

[37] *Bozkurt* was also the title of a Turanist, pan-Turkist magazine published in 1939–1940.

The *Ülkücü Organization in Belgium*

It is more pertinent to use the term Ülkücü than MHP, because the for-
mer refers to a grouping much larger than the MHP, which does not exist
officially in Belgium. It is the *Belçika Türk Federasyonu* (BTF, Turkish
Federation of Belgium in English; *Fédération turque de Belgique* in French;
Verbond der Turkse Verenigingen in België in Flemish) that represents the
Ülkücü Movement. The federation is organized in the three federal
regions of Belgium, in particular in Marchienne-au-Pont, Verviers, Liège,
Antwerp, Berchem, Brussels, and Ghent. The federation has branches of
youth, women's, and student organizations. Its associations are generally
referred to as Turkish hearth (or club), *Türk Ocağı*. *Ocak* is translated as
hearth, and also means fire or kitchen, and it metaphorically signifies
home. It constitutes the principal place of the Ülkücü and is charged with
Turkish cultural activities.

The reader can reasonably ask why I present this nationalist organization while this research deals mostly with religion among Turkish communities. The organization is part of the research because its activities
extend to the religious field. However, the federation cannot be handled
in the same as an Islamic federation because the primary finality of action
is not religious. There are three types of action which correspond to three
objectives. The central purpose is to promote the Turkish nationalist cause
and sentiments. As a member of the Turkish Federation of Europe, the
headquarters of which is in Germany, the organization organizes a con-
gress (*kurultay*) at both national and European levels, with other federal
members in Europe. One of the most remarkable activities consists of the
organization of demonstrations or celebrations about events that occur in
the Turkish world (not only in Turkey, but also in Central Asia or Turkish-
speaking communities in the Middle East).

A second purpose, linked with the first, is different as well because it
operates in a more reactionary way. It consists of building a public opinion
against the Kurdish and Armenian causes. The Belgian and international
contexts matter in this case: Belgium is a state that recognized the
Armenian question as genocide, which neither the Turkish government
nor the great majority of Turks consider to be true. They rather perceive
it as interethnic conflict or deportation of the Armenian people from
Anatolia during the First World War. It is thus a dynamic of differentiation
giving rise to conflict and Turkish nationalist mobilization. Furthermore,
the Kurdish diaspora is continually capable of mobilizing and consequently

triggering countermobilization of Turkish nationalists. Within this context, the Ülkücü Movement mobilizes in the street and organizes demonstrations, particularly when Kurdish or Armenian questions become more topical in Turkey or Belgium.

Third, some but not all activities have religious purposes. The federation manages roughly ten mosques and prayer houses. It has a funeral services fund called *Hilal Cenaze Fonu*. Similar to the Diyanet and Milli Görüş, there is organization for *Hac* or *Umre*. During the month of Ramadan, it organizes festivities and the communal meal(s) for breaking the fast. Thus, one notices that the federation is organized within the frame of some essential Islamic practices. At this point, a question which remains essential is: Why does a nationalist movement invest in the religious field?

Many factors can explain this investment. The first depends on the features and composition of the persons who constitute the group. Indeed, the Ülkücü Movement is formed by various individuals who occupy superior or subordinate positions within the movement. These people, all nationalist in nature, are divided in two groups: the first is nationalist and conservative, while the second group is nationalist, secularist, and Kemalist. In addition, there are two sorts of social base apportioned between nationalist Kemalism and religious nationalism. It seems that secular nationalism is less important in Belgium, as the majority of immigrants come from Central Anatolia. In Turkey, compared to Central Anatolia, people who support the Turkish nationalist movement in the Aegean, Mediterranean, and Marmara (Thrace) regions are less conservative and religious (this observation concerns only the comparison of the Ülkücü, and is not an integral comparison between these regions). However, Belgium has very few immigrants coming from the coastal regions of western Turkey which are characterized by greater economic prosperity. Furthermore, the competition with the AKP decreases the importance of this social base, as the AKP also mobilizes religious nationalism, resulting in the development of religious nationalism more than secular nationalism.[38]

[38] The rupture inside the MHP in Turkey gave rise to a new party in 2017, called *İyi Parti* (The Good Party, directed by Meral Akşener). The party won some supporters of the Grey Wolves in Belgium, showing that the break-up of the Turkish nationalist movement in Turkey impacted the nationalist social base in Belgium.

A second factor is linked with the effects of generation and historical conjuncture. The movement's formation in Belgium corresponds to the 1970s and 1980s, when the radical cleavage between the left and right wings was reigning within Turkish society. Conservative and religious members or sympathizers of the Ülkücü Movement perceived communism as atheism. Nationalist movements mobilized religious values and identity to frame society. The Ülkücü built prayer houses in Belgium during the 1970s and 1980s.

The third factor, perhaps most importantly, relates to mobilizing the power of religion. Religion is more than a spontaneous force, it is capable of mobilizing daily life, whereas nationalist causes like anti-Armenianism and anti-Kurdism are not always sufficient in mobilizing society, especially in Belgium. These motives simply do not have regularity. This argument goes beyond the analysis of Turkish nationalism but helps, at the same time, to explain why Islamic groups are capable of mobilizing their social bases. Indeed, social links between society and associative movements are constructed through religious and spiritual ties, which operate usually in holy places.

THE MENZİL BROTHERHOOD

The Nakşibendi is a Sufi brotherhood that was formed in the fourteenth and fifteenth centuries. It relies on the tradition of *tasawwuf*, a Muslim mystic system of thought. When it refers to a mystical Muslim current, it is Sufism. The Nakşibendi constitutes one of the most widespread Sufi movements in the Muslim world, especially in Central Asia and Turkey. Historically, it has been divided into two forms: *müceddidiye* and *hâlidiyye*. The origin of the *Nakşibendi müceddidiye* dates back to Sirhindi, also known as İmam-ı Rabbani by the Turks, a Muslim mystic thinker who lived in the sixteenth and seventeenth centuries in South Asia. As for *Nakşibendi hâlidiyye*, its name is derived from Mevlâna Hâlid-i Bağdâdi, who lived in the eighteenth and nineteenth centuries during the time of the Ottoman empire (in the current territories of Iraq and Syria). The *hâlidiyye* branch of Nakşibendi became widespread in Kurdistan (or Mesopotamia) and Anatolia, as well as in Syria under the leadership of Mevlâna Hâlid-i Bağdâdi.

The Menzil Brotherhood belongs to the *hâlidiyye* doctrine of Nakşibendi. The brotherhood's center is currently situated in Adıyaman, a Kurdish province in southeastern Turkey. The name Menzil comes from the Menzil village in Kâhta, a district in Adıyaman. Although Menzil is a geographic location, it also has a Sufi meaning: in the *tasawwuf, menzil* signifies the different degrees, stages of the journey, or spiritual pathways that humankind goes through in its quest for the Islamic truth (*hakikat*).[39] This brotherhood, like every other Nakşi order, legitimizes itself through its affiliation to the chain of order (*silsile*), which can be traced back from the current Sheikh to the Prophet of Islam. The relationship of the master with his disciples (*şeyh-mürid*) is fundamental to the group's constitution and affiliation; current followers are devoted to Gavs-ı Sani Şeyh Seyyid Abdulbaki, who resides in Menzil.

The Menzil Brotherhood is the most widespread *hâlidi* movement in Belgium as well as in Turkey and Europe. It has existed in Belgium since 1983. It was introduced and spread through the country by Yarbay, a charismatic individual about whom I will go into greater detail in Chap. 3. Yarbay, exiled to Germany, played an important role in the mobilization of the brotherhood in Europe. Menzil followers have associations in Belgium, but unlike the majority of the Muslim-Turkish movements, they do not have a mosque or imam within these associations. In everyday language, these organizations are often referred to as *vakıf,* or traditional mystic places such as *dergâh*, and *tekke*,[40] where people partake in Sufi activities.

Sufi practices are based on the concept of *seyr-i sülûk. Seyr* signifies the "course" or the "itinerary," and *sülûk* refers to the "journey." Thus, *seyr-i sülûk* literally means the "path" or the "travel route." The person who follows this route is called *sâlik, derviş,*[41] or *mürid*, who wants to become a perfect human being (*insan-ı kâmil*). His journey starts with the practice of *tevbe* (penance) and the *derviş, mürid*, or *sâlik* passes through states of being (*hal*). When a "state of being" is consolidated, it becomes a status, a *maqam*. The *seyr-i sülûk* encompasses different statuses to eliminate *nefs* (ego), a necessary condition to becoming the perfect being. In the Menzil Brotherhood, it is the level or "stage of the journey" (*mertebe*) at which the individual has arrived that shows his belonging to the brotherhood; there is a link between the *meşreb* (affiliation or identity; each degree also

---

[39] One can also translate *menzil* (*manzil* singular and *manâzil* plural in Arabic) as an "initiatory home" in English. Ibn al-ʿArabî uses the term quite frequently in his texts. See Ibn al-ʿArabî, *al-Futûhât al-Makkiyya* (9 volumes), Bayrût, Dâr al-Kutub al-ʿIlmiyyat, 1999.

[40] Tekke is a place where Muslim mystics gather.

[41] This is a Persian term meaning poor.

means a Menzil in Sufism), character, and morality with the status one achieves in Sufism.

Generally speaking, the internal practices can be summarized in two categories: the *vird* or *zikir*, and the conversation. *Zikir* means evocation or recall in Arabic. In Sufism, *zikir* relates to the different practices of the evocation of Allah. It is a rite aimed at leading a man or woman into a spiritual and sentimental state. In the *tarikat* orders, there exist two forms of *zikir*: the vocal *zikir* (*cehri*) and the silent *zikir* (*hafi*). One of the Menzil's characteristics is that it is a brotherhood that practices the silent *zikir*. When this *zikir* is exercised individually, it is *vird*. When it is done within a circle, it is called *hatme*.

The second category of practice is *sohbet* (conversation). Like *zikir*, the conversation may come in various forms, but the difference is that it is not a ritual; *sohbet*, which exists in all Muslim groups, is a form of exchange of words. It is an essential element that structures the religious habitus. A conversation can take place not only between the master and the *derviş*, but also among friends or *mürid* (disciples), meaning that it is not strictly hierarchical. It takes place within a circle where people are seated. The conversation may consist of query–response or rely on the diffusion and transmission of mystical knowledge and sentiments via stories and oral accounts, especially *menkıbes*.

All these mechanisms, which have practical and emotional aspects, generate a group of piety (*takva*) and asceticism (*zühd*). The general atmosphere in the circles is respect, sincerity, and mutual confidence. Even if Muslim organizations share a common semantic field, mystical orders (*tarikat*) have a more specific language. The Menzil disciples with whom I spoke on several occasions have a repertory of vocabulary, images, and metaphors such as *sır-ı hikmet* (secret wisdom), *kapı* (the door), *gavs* (a senior title attributed to the Sufi sheikh, which means the one who helps), *muhabbet* (love), and so on. To give an example among others, they sometimes use the expression "this door is open to everybody," which means that anyone can find the path of Menzil. The historical *menkıbes* create a common symbolic universe comprised of the various characters of *derviş*, *evliyas*, and *mürşid*. Sufis are trained to follow the same path as these historical figures.

Sufism is embedded within the field of religious faith, which addresses both the heart and the mind, according to Sufis. Menzil mysticism has created a socially shared imaginary and psychological identity. The identity is spread through imitation of the sheikh, *mürşid*, or *mürşid-i kâmil* by the *mürid* or *derviş* through the *menkıbe* or the sheikh's charisma. This diffusion generates pious behavior and spiritual emotions. These characteristics should not be understood merely as a simple description, but rather as a sense of the community (*tarikat*) which is based on these values and practices.

SHIISM AND THE TURKS

General Aspects of Shiism and Its Geographic Distribution Among the Turks in Belgium

Shiism constitutes an Islamic denomination, the followers of which have a particular attachment to Imam Ali, son-in-law and cousin of the Prophet, and to members of *Ehl-i Beyt* (the Prophet's family). This attachment generated a different conception of successor as Islamic leadership and political authority after the death of the Prophet and gave rise to some religious rituals specific to Shiism. These divergences were not merely the outcome of different points of view between Sunni and Shia Muslims, but also they developed through historical facts: the most important was the fact that the Shiites favored the right of the successor (Muslim caliph) belonging to a member of the Prophet's family, while the Sunnis preferred to elect a successor. A full discussion of the differences between Shiism and Sunnism lies beyond the scope of this study. I will refer to them when it is necessary to explain certain essential points of my research.

Shiites represent about 10 percent of the Muslim population throughout the world. Iran, Iraq, and Bahrain's populations are majority Shiite, while Yemen, Afghanistan, Pakistan, and Lebanon have important Shia minority communities. Azerbaijan is a unique Turkic-speaking country (Azeri belonging to the Turkic language category) where the majority of the population is Shiite.

In contemporary Turkey, the Shiites, who are a minority as well, mainly come from the eastern provinces, in particular Kars and Iğdır.[42] Shiism is more widespread among the Turkmen (or the Azeri) who live near the

---

[42] Istanbul also harbors part of the Shia community, as people immigrated from Kars and Iğdır.

Iranian border (Turkmen[43] are a Turkish sub-ethnic group). This geographic specificity also explains why Shiism is present among Turks living in Belgium as well. The topic of Shiism indeed enables us to underline a significant fact: the composition of ethnic and confessional groups among the Turks and Kurds in Belgium depends on particularities regarding the places of origin of the people who come from Anatolia. The researcher should take into account this geographic aspect, which has a temporal dimension, to explain the presence of religious communities in Belgium. For example, people coming from Afyon do not manifest the same ethnic, social, and confessional characteristics as people coming from Iğdır, although they share certainly common points. The difference in religious denomination at times coincides with a different ethnicity, sub-ethnicity, or regionalization.[44] Turkish-speaking people who immigrated from the Caucasus are part of this Shia community as well.[45] They are usually Turkmen and Azeri sub-ethnic communities. The Shiites with whom I conducted interviews generally showed a strong dual sense of belonging to both the Turkish identity and Shiism.

How is the Turkish Shia community geographically distributed in Belgium? There is no statistical data or document providing this information. Based on my field investigations, Brussels harbors most of the Turkish Shiites, together with Beringen, Genk, Maasmechelen, and Antwerp. Since they constitute a quantitatively small minority community compared to the Sunnis, cultural and economic solidarity characterizes their members. It is possible to observe endogamous marriages as well as solidarity in economic affairs such as the catering, construction, and industrial sectors among the Shiites. This community maintains relations with non-Turkish-speaking Shia communities like the Lebanese and Turkish Shiites in Europe, particularly in the Netherlands.

The Shiites also are organized around the mosques from religious and social perspectives. There are at least ten Turkish Shia associations in Belgium, which are mostly in Brussels, Genk, and Beringen. Associations, founded according to the local dynamics of the Shia community in the

---

[43] The use of the term Turkmen is at times contested by scholars, who argue that the term is not appropriate to distinguish historically the majority of Anatolian Turks and Turks living in Syria, Iraq and Central Asia.

[44] This is also what I noted about the Turkish and Kurdish Alevis and would perhaps apply to other cases.

[45] The Turkish community in Belgium extends to the Balkan countries and the Caucasus, despite the majority coming from Anatolia.

region concerned, seem to operate autonomously with each other. But, as stated above, collective solidarity among the Shia population gives rise to cooperation and exchange at the national (Belgian) and trans-regional levels (between the Shia communities in Belgium and the Netherlands). Every mosque has a Shiite imam who plays the key role in the organization of religious rituals and activities.

To clarify the specificity of this community, it is pertinent to underline that Shiism is characterized by different movements. The majority of the Turkish Shia population belongs to Caferism (or Jafarism in English). It is a duodecimal doctrine (*ithna 'ashara*), which constitutes the most widespread Shia movement. Shia movements differ from each other according to divergent genealogy and the lineage of the imams. For the Twelvers (duodecimal Shiism), the succession of the imams terminates with the twelfth imam; whereas, for example, for the Septimanian or Ismailis, the lineage terminates with the seventh imam. For the Caferis in general, including Turkish-speaking Caferis, the twelfth imam, Mahdi, is the hidden imam, the returning of whom will bring the reign of peace, justice, and Islamic truth.

This being said, which is also believed by the Sunni people but in a less nuanced or central way, it is relevant to outline the Turkish Shia community's ritual practices and social activities in Belgium.

In general, the activities of Shia associations are similar to those of Sunni organizations. The daily prayer is the principal ritual in the mosque of the Shiites, like the mosque of the Sunnis. Fasting is practiced during Ramadan, a period in which religious practices intensify. Fasting is also practiced during the month of Muharram (a term derived from the root *harama*, meaning forbidden), which is the first month of the Islamic calendar.

Distinct from Hanafism, which characterizes most of the mosques affiliated with the Sunni Turks, Shia imams follow the Caferi conception of *fiqh* (jurisprudence) and science of *kalâm*. The detailed differences between the two judicial and philosophical conceptions (Caferism and Hanafism) go beyond this research. They are not simple religious thought differences given that they influence the rules, modalities of practices regarding the rituals, rights, prohibitions, and activities occurring within the religious frame. For example, the Shiites organize the ceremonies of Karbala to commemorate the different sessions of *mâtem* (mourning or grief) and *mersiye* (elegy) during the month of Muharram in Belgium, because Imam Hüseyin was killed in Kerbela on the tenth day of Muharram (the year

61 in the Islamic lunar calendar, or the year 680 in the Gregorian calendar). This day of celebration is commonly referred to as *aşure günü* in Turkish. The social and cultural fields are also characterized by similar activities in Sunni communities: there are identical sports and festive activities, like the Kermes, as presented above. The people who participate in these activities are different, however, because the Shia population of Belgium includes Shia Turks, Azeris, and Lebanese who organize the activities. The Erenler, an Alevi group (as discussed below), supports and participates in certain activities, because it is a religious group close to Shiism. I noticed on the other hand some cultural singularities like the feast of Nevruz, which is organized by Shia who come from eastern Anatolia. It is a celebration of the arrival of spring on March 21, organized also by the Kurds and the Persians in their associations, but not by the Turks who come from Central Anatolia. Nevruz brings people together, but the feast is not of a religious nature.

THE ALEVIS

Alevism is a minority[46] in Islam. The term Alevi generally designates people or communities attached to Imam Ali, son-in-law of the Prophet, and to *Ehl-i Beyt* (the family of the Prophet). Alevism is a religious movement close to Shiism, at least due to its origin, but because of the divergence of religious practices and Alevi way of life throughout history, it would be fruitful to avoid qualifying today's Alevism as a branch of Shiism. Alevism may have developed among nomadic or semi-nomadic Turkic peoples, who immigrated from Central Asia to Anatolia during the Seljuk and Ottoman periods.

The appellation bektashism (or *bektâshiyya*), usually tied to Alevism, draws its name from Hacı Bektaş-ı Veli (thirteenth century) and was institutionalized in Anatolia by Balım Sultan (?–1516). Bektashism developed as a *tarikat* within Alevism, but they should not be used as interchangeable terms. The philosophy of Hacı Bektaş-ı Veli as well as other similar figures like Pir Sultan Abdal (sixteenth century) served as a common

---

[46] Orientalism judges Alevism as heterodox. Heterodoxy and orthodoxy are terms used in Christianity. Their use within other religions should be clarified. One can employ the term heterodoxy only in a sociological sense to signify the minority aspect of the Alevi confession.

framework of reference for Alevism, which is founded upon mysticism and love for humankind. *Kızılbaş* (which signifies "red head" in Turkish) is another term employed at times to designate the Alevis, referring to the partisans of Shia Safavids who wore red head coverings in the sixteenth century. The progressive institutionalization of Sunni authority and the Ottoman's political and military victory against the Shia Safavid empire resulted in the marginalization of the Alevi community in Anatolia. This process did not interrupt republican Turkey, because the modern state favored the Sunni conception. Nowadays, between fifteen and twenty million Alevis are estimated to live in Turkey. They belong to both Turkish and Kurdish ethnicities and live in areas such as Dersim, Erzincan, Maraş, Bingöl, Adıyaman, Malatya (in the east and southeast of the country), Çorum, Sivas, Mersin, Edirne, and Istanbul.

Organization of Alevism in Belgium

Belgium currently harbors about 35,000 Alevis. The context of immigration needs to be clarified, because it differs from other communities' immigration in Belgium. Alevis coming from Afyon immigrated to Belgium in the 1960s and 1970s; namely, at the same time as the Sunni population's immigration from Turkey to Belgium. There are other processes of displacement of the Alevis from Turkey to Belgium, such as the Alevi massacre at Maraş, a Kurdish Turkish province, in 1978 and the massacre at Gâzi, a popular district in Istanbul, in 1995. Such violent processes impacted the community in Turkey, part of whom eventually immigrated to Europe.

The Alevis began to organize in Belgium in the 1970s. This mobilization resulted in the establishment of associations in the region of Limbourg, Brussels, Charleroi, and Liège. At present, the Alevi organization is gathered around a federation called *Belçika Alevi Birlikleri Federasyonu* (Union Federation of the Alevis in Belgium; *Fédération Union des Alevis de Belgique* in French; *Federatie van Belgische Alevitische Verenigingen* in Flemish), founded in 2003. It is located in Brussels and includes five Alevi cultural centers in Antwerp, Liège, Charleroi, Brussels, and Verviers. These regions also are the places where the majority of the Alevi population who immigrated live, particularly those from the Turkish and Kurdish provinces and the Balkan countries. On the other hand, two types of Alevi associations differ from the federation and are not part of it.

The first is the Alevi association Erenler, an organization established by Alevis coming from the village of Karacalar (located in Emirdağ, Afyon) and directed by the family of Şahbaz, a native of this village for a long time. The Erenler has two cultural centers, one in Brussels[47] and one in Ghent. The migrant community from the Karacalar village, who lives in Brussels and Ghent, demonstrates social solidarity (endogamous marriages, common commercial activities, gathering and visiting places, etc.) and is perhaps more knitted and cohesive than the community of Emirdağ, because it is smaller and thus fosters collective action. When members of a small social group immigrate together from one place to another, they have the capacity to fulfill the social, cultural, and psychological needs of members in this new place. This is more apparent when most of the people personally know each other.

The second type of non-partisan association of the Alevi federation is the Kurdish Alevi organization located in Verviers, oriented by Kurdish nationalism. The Alevi population thus does not constitute a homogenous community from either a social or associative aspect in Belgium. When the Alevis are asked, they generally identify themselves with different historical moments, and different social and ethnic factors. Some of them promote the Alevi identity, while others closely identify themselves with Kemalism; others mobilize the Kurdish cause or the radical left, and consequently act independently from each other, even in opposite ways.[48]

Alevism is also present in certain segments of Turkish-speaking communities who immigrated from the Balkans, in particular Bulgaria. However, the fact that people from the Balkans are Alevi-Bektaşi does not necessarily lead to association. There are sometimes religious elements which determines men's and women's identities. Although these elements are categories of action which belong in individual and daily lives, they do not automatically give rise to a social organization capable of defending the mutual interests of a particular group.

---

[47] Michaël Lebrecht, *Alévis en Belgique. Approche générale et étude de cas*, Brussels, Academia-Bruylant, 1997.

[48] For example, in addition to common figures and historical events such as the event of Karbala and Pir Sultan Abdal among the Alevis, the revolt of Koçgiri and the massacres of Dersim and Maraş occupy a place in the collective imaginary of the Alevi Kurds, which is not the case among the Turkish Alevis.

Alevi Ritual Practices and Cultural Activities in Belgium

Alevi practices have particularities from the point of view of organization, form, and content. The central religious place is called *cem evi* (literally "house of meeting"; *cem* signifies "assembly" in Arabic and *ev* is "home" or "house" in Turkish). The *dede* (literally grandfather in Turkish) or the *pir* (old man in Kurdish and Farsi) is the central figure of both religious and social mobilization: he holds an authority which organizes Alevism. When *dede* (or *pir*) is absent, the Alevism faces difficulties mobilizing, which is perhaps the case for Alevism in Belgium. I will continue to discuss this topic in Chap. 3. Below are the principal Alevi activities.

Cem is the Alevi's principal ritual, which takes place under the leadership of a *dede*. There are different hierarchized practices in the *cem*, a detailed explanation of which would go beyond the scope of this study. *Cem*'s essential root is found in the *kırklar cemi* or "assembly of the 40s." For the Alevis, this is a symbolic ritual of *cem* which refers to the assembly of the 40 saints. The assembly of the 40s corresponds to an event which is believed to have taken place during the period of the first Muslim community in Medina and is interpreted in different ways, over which there is not consensus between the Sunnis and the Alevis. Another religious practice performed by the Alevis is fasting, especially during the month of Muharram, the moment at which Imam Hüseyin[49] was killed in 680. Different from the fasting during the month of Ramadan, practiced by the Sunnis, it lasts twelve days.

Music constitutes another repertoire of action which is both religious and cultural to the Alevis. The *semah* is a religious ritual performed by rhythmic words during the procedure of *cem*. It is indeed a session of dance where men and women turn around, accompanied by a music played with a *saz*, an instrument that is a long-necked lute.

There are also specific political and social motives which differentiate the field of Alevi action. An important part of the collective action conducted by the Alevi associations in Belgium aims at the recognition of Alevism, which is a religious minority, but this demand is especially oriented toward Turkey, and is not necessarily or exclusively in Belgium. This is one of the differences from Turkish Sunni groups who claim so few demands vis-à-vis the Turkish government. (This aspect should not be

---

[49] Imam Hüseyin was the son of Imam Ali and the grandson of the Prophet of Islam. He was killed in Karbala by the army of the Umayyad dynasty. Karbala, located in Iraq, is one of the holy places of Shiism and is located in Iraqi territory.

confused with the network extending to the native country, an important issue which will be handled in Chap. 3). Moreover, Kurdish Alevi associations mobilize in favor of the Kurdish cause and engage in protest acts against the Turkish government, more than they conduct Alevi-oriented rituals and activities. In addition, there are political activities conducted by the Alevis who are involved in the Turkish radical left and have refugee status in Belgium; they do not claim a religious cause. These activities undertaken by the Alevis, involved in the Kurdish movement or Turkish left groups, show the shift of the Alevi cause toward ethnic or political motivations.

CHAPTER 3

Islamic Movement, Mobilization, and Authority

Abstract This chapter analyzes the formation of associations by Turkish Islamic communities. Islamic mobilization relies on traditional, charismatic, and bureaucratic powers that operate through the dynamics of proximity and distance. Proximity has a diversity of relations enacted by multiple figures of religious authority in the mosque, the association, or the neighborhood. The distance shows multiple levels of political, religious, cultural, or symbolic connections to the native country and the Muslim world. Islamic rituals, characteristics of movements and communities, and their spheres of mobilization shape the forms of proximity and distance. Such a complex mobilization persists due to the permanence of religious rituals and practices in accordance with Islamic temporality.

Keywords Religion • Proximity • Distance • Territoriality • Temporality

INTRODUCTION

This chapter aims to examine Islamic mobilization, movement, and authority in Turkish communities and associations. Chapter 2, despite being dedicated to the overview of Islamic movements, does not shed sufficient light on these themes. The framework and questions that the present chapter attempts to study are as follows. The chapter begins with

© The Author(s) 2020   55
M. Orhan, *Islam and Turks in Belgium*, New Directions in Islam,
https://doi.org/10.1007/978-3-030-34655-3_3

an ethnographic and historical description of Houthalen and Verviers to explore the mechanisms of Turkish and Muslim mobilization. I chose these two sites to describe, among other observations, because they present different socio-economic and linguistic characteristics in Belgium. Houthalen is located in Flemish-speaking Flanders, and it is more prosperous than French-speaking Verviers, situated in Wallonia. I combined the knowledge about these two local contexts with the research data in other Belgian localities. The observation of multiple sites of movements is a methodological procedure that enables a response to the following question in the first step: Why and how did the Turks start to mobilize?

The chapter will then continue to discuss how this mobilization evolves. The introductory examples, provided at the beginning of the chapter, deal with the construction of places of worship in Wallonia and Flanders. While indicative of Muslim action involving religious, cultural, and identity mechanisms, these examples are not totally independent from the questions addressed in this chapter: Who are the traditional authority figures who exist through this type of primary mobilization? What are the links between the social base and these religious figures? Are the titles and roles convergent or divergent between religious communal groups? Focusing on such issues will develop the following central question: If traditional actors are structured within communities (*cemaat, tarikat, mezheb*), to what extent does the association (*cemiyet*), a new form of power, produce new lines of action and mobilization without excluding traditional authority?

The Case of the Yeşil Camii Mosque in Houthalen-Helchteren

Houthalen-Helchteren is a municipality situated in the province of Limburg in Flanders. It has a population of nearly 35,000 people, of whom 4000 are immigrants of Turkish origin. The process of the Yeşil Camii mosque's construction offers a relevant case when examining religious mobilization. The methodology used in the Houthalen case study combines two processes: the first consists of a text analysis published by the Executive Board of the Yeşil Camii mosque, based on mosque archives. The second method is ethnographic research. As explained earlier, this is the principal method of this study. Nonetheless, since the brochure published by the mosque contains more comprehensive and systematic information on the construction process of Yeşil Camii, this historical case is built in large part on textual data interpretation. This chapter is not exclusively based on

Houthalen, as it is a study concerning the whole of Belgium. It is not intended to construct themes and develop hypotheses while limiting the discussion to a single religious medium. It is, however, essential to provide specific examples in qualitative research. Additional examples will be provided as the study continues to examine religious mobilization.

"The Houthalen-Helchteren region attracted Turkish and Muslim immigrants from the early 1960s onward because of its coal mines. The early settlers took up residence in the Meulenberg district, which is now densely populated with Turkish immigrants. Instead of spreading out into different streets, most of the workers lived on Groot Baan street, where a Turkish café was later established as a social venue for the men. This café was run by two workers who were among the founders of the Yeşil Camii mosque. In the 1970s, the workers brought their families from Turkey, a process which caused a relocation from public housing to private dwellings. This occurred for two reasons: the housing projects were equipped with canteens that did not prepare food in accordance with Muslim norms; and these new private housing units provided them with a more autonomous lifestyle. At that time, there was no mosque in Houthalen. The workers prayed in a mosque named Selimiye Camii that was built in Heusden-Lindeman at the request of the Turkish workmen in 1963. Once the population size increased, the Turkish community built a mosque in Houthalen.

Initially, they asked the mayor for a piece of land on which they could build the mosque, and then established a fund financed by the Turkish community in 1975. In the meantime, an association of Turkish workmen rented a cabin and transformed it into a prayer room in 1977. A year later, the mayor of Houthalen designated a piece of land for the construction of the mosque on Saviostraat street, where the Yeşil Camii mosque is currently located. Since this land was predominantly covered by poplars and pines, the Turkish workers named the mosque the Green Mosque (*yeşil* in Turkish). Turkish workers in Houthalen became increasingly aware of the declining possibility of returning to Turkey in the 1980s, more than in the 1970s. This awareness explains the purchase of this land from the municipality for the amount of 800,000 Belgian francs and the construction of a mosque. They transferred it to the Diyanet foundation in Belgium in 1986.

Two key figures emerged in the 1970s in Houthalen: the imam and the teacher. Both were part of this process, not as leaders in the mosque's construction, but rather in a parallel manner. The imam, with his religious knowledge, conducted the prayers in the mosque, and the teacher transmitted the Turkish language and culture in the school. (The teacher has cultural legitimacy whereas the imam has religious legitimacy.) From the 1960s to the 1990s, two parallel trends occurred: the growth of Turkish and the rise of a young generation participating in mosque activities. Between 1995 and 1998, the mosque was rebuilt to what it is today, except the minaret, which would be constructed later on. The Flemish government issued a decree recognizing mosques in 2004. This mosque was officially recognized by the federal government in 2009. The mosque association formally requested from the Houthalen municipality that two minarets be constructed. This process is significant in terms of intercommunal conflict because of the local backlash it caused, at the initiative of *Vlaams Belang*,[1] which was already conducting a campaign against the construction of the mosque. The Swiss referendum of 2009, prohibiting the construction of minarets, also influenced the context. Thus, close to 300 signatures were collected to prevent the construction of minarets in Houthalen. But despite these three countermovements at the local, national, and international levels, the town council accepted one of the two minarets. A minaret, transported by truck from Turkey, was consequently added to the mosque in 2010."[2]

Maurice Halbwachs' observation about the relationship between a social group and the space it inhabits is applicable to the Houthalen case: when a community or even an individual occupies part of a space, they reshape it in accordance with their culture, memory, religion, identity, or image:[3] "But at the same time, they adjust and adapt to the material elements that remain resistant. They enclose themselves inside the framework they constructed."[4]

The Case of Verviers

Verviers is a French-speaking city located in the Walloon region with nearly 60,000 inhabitants. A large portion of the population is Muslim, including at least 4000 Turkish speakers. The development of the mining industry and the wool trade caused migration to the city in the nineteenth and twentieth centuries. Initially the migrants came from rural areas sur-

---

[1] A radical right-wing Flemish political party.

[2] Yeşil Camii Houthalen, *40 yıl Yeşil Camii, Houthalen-Helchteren*, Date unknown. This extended quote relies on a translation from the source mentioned in this footnote, mixed with my ethnographic observations in Houthalen.

[3] Maurice Halbwachs, *La mémoire collective*, Paris, PUF, 1950, p. 132.

[4] Halbwachs, *op.cit.*, p. 132.

rounding Verviers or from Germany because of the geographic proximity, but the origin of the migrants changed with the arrival of the Turks, Moroccans, Somalians, and Chechens in the second half of the twentieth century. Following is a brief socio-historical overview of the Muslim mobilization, which offers additional accounts to analyze contemporary religious power among the Turks in Belgium.[5]

The Turks started to immigrate to Verviers around 1964 upon an agreement signed between the Belgian and Turkish governments. A few immigrants migrated before this date, namely Turks who arrived earlier in Germany and settled down in Verviers to work. The new immigrants were young, single men or those who had left their family in Turkey in order to work, earn money, and then return there. Because there were almost only men at that time, this community was not a social group divided between the sexes. The specificity of this small community was instrumental in the formation of sociability in the area. In the 1960s, the immigrant workers used to frequent Greek cafés. Having no family or social places similar to their original culture, they sought to build their social circle, namely through meeting at these cafés. These were places without any religious connection and it was the ethno-cultural dynamic which allowed the men to come together and converse, drink tea, and play dominoes. In this way, the first Turkish café was opened in the early 1970s. The Turkish men who worked in the local plants, mines, and textile workshops gathered in this café, which was relatively autonomous from places in the Greek, Italian, or Belgian style. This café was the sole meeting point for Turkish immigrants and lured even the Turkish workmen who worked and lived 10–15 kilometers outside Verviers. In 1975, the Turkish cafés started to multiply. Around the same time, family reunifications brought about changes which affected community development in quantitative and qualitative terms. Turkish men started getting married or bringing their wives, children, or other relatives from Turkey to Belgium. Nowadays, when walking around the city center, it is common to see Turkish men and women who were born in the 1970s, or even those who came there as children with their fathers.

This process needs to be explained rather than taken for granted, because the arrival of the women, and especially children, drives the men to better build their religious circles. Such was the case with Verviers

---

[5] I collected the information about Verviers through group interviews and discussions with Muslims in Verviers.

(although this was not the only dynamic: the workers, who were without children, were also worried about not having a place of worship after their arrival in Belgium). The worshippers prayed either in a room reserved for prayer in the café or in their homes. A group of men told me a significant anecdote: one day, an old man entered the café where they were and asked if there was a mosque in Verviers, and where the people prayed. This question gave them the idea of establishing an association and place of worship in Verviers. The first nonprofit association was created in the mid-1970s. There was a prayer room in the association's building. As this place lacked sufficient space, the followers relocated three times before founding the current mosque of Orhan Gazi, located on rue des Messieurs. The social and physical construction of the mosque spanned over three decades (from the 1970s to 2000s) before the mosque took its current form. This is a historical process quite similar to what happened in Houthalen. The actors who built it are identical: they were migrant workers from various rural Anatolian villages.

Verviers suffered from an economic crisis in the 1980s, induced by the oil price shocks in 1973 and 1979, but mostly due to closure of the industrial plants and textile shops. This created unemployment within the Turkish community and led people to search for employment in other sectors. Thus, sectors like construction and the restaurant business progressively emerged, thereby giving rise to a small bourgeoisie among the Turks. One may add the pensioners' category to this social class, given that the workers who settled there in the 1960s started to retire in the 1980s. They retired early because of the severe working conditions they were exposed to during their lives. All of these social classes actively participated in the construction of the Orhan Gazi mosque, which necessitated a local economy, public investment, and a labor force. Just like in other Belgian villages, the workers built the mosque and bought it before transferring it to the Diyanet. Following the emergence of the Ülkücü, Milli Görüş, and Süleymanlı movements in Verviers, three more mosques were built toward the end of the 1980s. The Turkish community currently has four mosques in Verviers. Despite the competition, the relationship between the movements is peaceful.

It is worth noting that the religious movements became more diverse from the 1980s, due to two main factors. First, there are structural differences among the immigrant communities. For example, Turkish Alevis founded an Alevi association, whereas refugees or Kurdish immigrants mobilized the Kurds, including Alevi and Sunni Kurds, through a cultural association. Secondly, this diversification is linked to the religious and political fields in the Muslim world. This is best exemplified by the *Refah Partisi* (Welfare Party). It seems that the rise of the Refah in Turkey favored the organization of the Milli Görüş in Verviers during the 1990s. This case is not generalizable, since the mobilization of the Milli Görüş had already started in the 1970s and 1980s in Brussels and Antwerp, as was the case in Germany. *Refah*'s success drove the Turks to support the Milli Görüş movement in Verviers. The *Refah* movement in Turkey also impacted the society in Verviers on a cultural level. Muslim women adopted a new style of headscarf and modest wear in the public space by wearing overcoats—long-sleeved garments—in the late 1980s and the early 1990s in Verviers. Until then, they wore traditional clothes with a headscarf. This change in cultural behavior was driven by three elements: the capitalist urbanization of the Anatolian community in Verviers; the influence of the *Refah Partisi* (an Islamic party that was active between 1983 and 1998 in Turkey) over the Muslim society in Verviers; and lastly the esthetic choices of women which are at the same time determined by male preferences. The change occurred simultaneously in an esthetic and religious setting. The AKP (Justice and Development Party) rapidly became very popular following its seizure of power in the 2000s, but unlike the Refah, it did not set off a new movement. However, the AKP, together with its founder Recep Tayyip Erdoğan, is greatly appreciated in Verviers and within the Turkish population in Belgium in general.

An important comment should be made regarding the municipal elections in Verviers (among various other examples in Belgium and Europe), the latest of which took place in 2012. The growth of Turkish and Muslim populations led to the success of Muslim candidates. Candidates of Turkish origin began to enter the electoral lists in the late 1990s in Belgium. Emir Kır, the current mayor at Saint-Josse, a district in Brussels, became the first elected mayor of Turkish origin in Europe. As for Verviers, Hasan Aydın, a candidate of Turkish origin from the Socialist Party, was elected municipal councilor with 1545 votes in 2012.[6] Aside from the quality of such candidates, the possession of social capital—namely, having good relations

---

[6] In general, Turkish-speaking candidates stand for election under the Socialist Party (*Parti Socialiste* in French) and the Christian Democratic Party in Flanders (*Christen-Democratisch en Vlaams* in Flemish). In the municipal elections of 2012, 355 candidates born to immigrant parents from Turkey ran for election, and 104 of them were elected in Brussels, Wallonia, and Flanders. http://www.binfikir.be/2012/10/14/secilen-turklerin-tam-listesi/

with their community and leading a campaign focused on its everyday problems—is an important factor that drove people to vote for them. In addition, the fact that the majority of their votes come from the Turkish and Muslim communities shows that the candidates' origin seems to play a considerable role in the political choices made by migrant communities in Verviers or in Belgium.

THE MUSLIM MOBILIZATION

The cases of Verviers and Houthalen, along with other neighborhoods and villages, have provided fruitful examples for studying the formation of religious power, the different contemporary aspects of which processes this chapter aims to develop. This social, cultural, and religious power relies on popular mobilization, which has been taking place since the 1960s and 1970s. The phenomenon of mobilization is a vast concept which applies to different situations, such as civil war, physical conflict, revolution, and social movements. Here the concept refers to the capacity of collective action by religious groups and communities. It is not synonymous with power, but rather power takes the form of the medium, especially because mobilization is linked to the making of collective action and Muslim communities which constitute and establish power. Mobilization is therefore a key notion to understand power and authority.

The cases of Houthalen and Verviers should not be understood as exceptional examples, although each case naturally presents specific traits that are unique to each different scenario. The empirical variety results from the richness of the real world, but unfortunately it is not possible to specify the characteristics of each field due to practical constraints.[7] Identifying common mechanisms, however, enables an understanding of the phenomenon under study. Here I consider the religious process as a general progression which is formed by a complex combination of social episodes and local processes.[8] These processes do not necessarily take place

---

[7] The method of observation and the issue in question are not exactly identical, but the example provided by Ural Manço and Meryem Kanmaz is similar to the historical cases presented here. Ural Manço and Meryem Kanmaz, "From Conflict to Co-operation Between Muslims and Local Authorities in a Brussels Borough: Schaerbeek", *Journal of Ethnic and Migration Studies*, Vol. 31, No. 6, 2005, pp. 1105–1123.

[8] He does not study the religious fact, but my conception of the historical process is due to Charles Tilly. See Tilly, *From Mobilization to Revolution*, Reading, MA: Addison-Wesley, 1978.

through recurrent forms, but in various aspects which evolve and change over time.[9] Antwerp, Brussels, Marchienne-au-Pont, Charleroi, and Liège, among others, are added to these local episodes and processes. In this context, it is worthwhile to consider the following questions: What do these cumulative processes result in? What are the common traits of these local mobilizations?

The first characteristic lies in the fact that the Turkish immigrants are peasants turned proletarians. Although the social classes became more varied because of the emergence of a bourgeoisie and a middle class in the 1990s, a factor which considerably influenced the religious mobilization due to the economic contribution of these new social classes, the Turkish community still consists mostly of laborers, local shopkeepers, and artisans. In the 1960s and 1970s, they were members of a social class stemming from the rural peasantry, made up of immigrants escaping the economic crisis in Anatolia; a crisis that progressively transitioned into a social crisis in Belgium. Indeed, the workers went through a cultural confrontation. A man told me that for the very first time he had seen a woman who could ride a bike in Verviers; others experienced trains for the first time. These examples should not be misinterpreted: it is not the woman on the bike or the train which triggers the religious quest. Regardless, my informants who brought up these examples were not against the train or the fact that a woman rides a bike. These accounts demonstrate how much their socio-cultural and economic worlds differed. Maybe remarks such as "We did not like Greek cafés in Verviers" or "the canteen of social apartments was the cause for renting private accommodation in Houthalen" are more relevant from a religious viewpoint, because these were places in which their religious and cultural norms were not exercised. This was one of the reasons why Turkish immigrants started to build places of worship informally. These places of religious worship were found first in coffee shops, dwellings, or cabins. These findings suggest that a poor social class who are attached to the Islamic faith remain concerned about affirming their belonging to a social and cultural entity, as well as to the different religious movements, in order to defend their ideological interests, more than their material interests. They indicate that, among the immigrants, there is a fear of detaching from their belief, their original culture, and uprooting themselves, which triggers collective action that is also central in the formation of religious groups and circles. The protec-

[9] Tilly, *From Mobilization to Revolution.*

tion of one's self, faith, and identity results in mobilization. This notion indicates that the main motive of history and society is conservation. Minority communities' rationality is apparent here. With that in mind, the actors use economic or symbolic resources, such as language or communal ties. However, this quest for protection sometimes does not exclude an identity-related affirmation and more visible faith, which gives rise to a certain moderate social conflict between Muslims and non-Muslims, as already seen in the example of the minaret in Houthalen.

This process lies within the experience of subjectivity. It is the religious and ethnic structure which determines the men and women who confront another culture.

There is also a mechanism which explains how collective religious action starts at a local level, and manifests in action at the national level: the change in scale. A clarification is needed as to what constitutes this mechanism. It empirically corresponds to the creation of federations and unions, including the associations which operate at the national level in this study. The change in scale is the product of several cumulative and local processes. It was not collective religious action which appeared in a specific place and spread to other places by conscious or unconscious imitation.[10] Rather, there were movements which were set off simultaneously in similar places, under similar conditions. To speak more concretely, the building of mosques and the foundation of associations did not start in a unique place. It was a movement which began in various localities where Turkish immigrants lived. However, once people created federations and unions of associations, such as the Diyanet and the Islamic Federation of Belgium (BIF), these associations progressively organized the power around these federations and unions of associations. A clear example of this is seen within the framework of a project to build a mosque, an association, or a school. None of these is independent from popular and local dynamics. Hence, there are religious movements which have a dual capacity for action: it is both horizontal mobilization, namely a movement from top to bottom; and vertical mobilization, that is, a movement from the bottom up.

This mobilization process becomes all the more complex when the associations and federations interact with municipal and federal govern-

---

[10] In the work by Charles Tilly and Sydney Tarrow, this process applies to a social movement which emerges relatively more rapidly, whereas the mobilization here is slow and less spontaneous. Tilly and Tarrow, *Politique(s) du conflit*, Paris, Presses de Sciences Po, 2008.

mental institutions. Federations, associations, and the subsequent actions of these actors between local and national authorities play out in different ways, which leads to difficulties in making generalizations. Earlier, I interpreted the question of the minaret construction in Houthalen in terms of religion and identity within an intercultural and societal context. This context is itself very moving. Such questions also involve an aspect linked to the power relations between the association and the local and federal authority determined by Belgian law. For example, what is authorized by Belgian law? What is the scope for interpretation of this law and the procedures of the approach that are part of these power relations? Indeed, the process of collective action is determined to some extent by the legal framework. In the same way, the construction of new schools and mosques involves multiple economic, political, and legal power relations which are shaped by several actors and factors. Therefore, it is sometimes methodologically more reasonable to discuss a case for an analysis rather than to schematize the whole of relations in a rigid way.

The educational institute of Houthalen, which has the objective of religious education for imams, as mentioned in Chap. 2, offers an example for a case study. Indeed, this investment of the Diyanet falls concurrently within a societal, Belgian, and international context, which involves both the constraint and the will of the actors. The institute was born as a necessity. The Muslim population has experienced European culture for decades, requiring imams to know the context in its cultural and linguistic dimensions. The construction of the educational institute of Houthalen differs from the Yeşil Camii mosque in Houthalen: the mosque was built by the community which transferred its property to the Diyanet, whereas the project of building this educational institute was initiated by the Diyanet and supported by the Turkish community. Building such an institute is a response both to the implicit request of the Belgian government and, more generally, to the current European debate, which claims that the training of religious personnel should be carried out within Europe.

In short, religious mobilization is motivated by the protection of self, of faith, and of identity. Religious mobilization is enhanced particularly by the fact that Muslims are a minority in Europe. This motivation is the principal dynamic of various cumulative processes simultaneously initiated on a local level, which lead to a change in scale. These two complementary processes, namely subjective and organizational, give rise to the construction of a complex power which is essential to understand the development of religious movements.

ISLAM AND TRADITIONAL POWER

The power is traditional when it is based on everyday popular belief and the sacredness of practices carried out since ancient times, and the legitimacy of those who exercise authority through traditional means.[11] In this case, the power is linked to past precedents.[12] We can therefore identify two aspects which form this type of power. The first relates to religious rituals and practices which are the basis of Muslim tradition. The second aspect concerns the authority figures traditionally expected to run and exercise religious practices with the participation of worshippers. In Sunnite and Shiite Islam (not only among the Turks, but also among other Muslim people), prayer is the pillar of religion.[13] There is neither *râhib* (monk) nor *rahbâniyya* (monasticism),[14] which means, according to Muslim belief, that there is no clergy to act as an intermediary between the individual and God. The principal traditional authority figure is connected to the practice of ritual prayer in the mosque. It is the imam who conducts the prayer and, therefore, constitutes a central authority figure. This is all the more important because the principal Turkish movements such as the Diyanet, the Milli Görüş, and the Shiites manage the mosques (see the discussion in Chap. 2). It is necessary to specify this authority: it is not just the imam who constitutes the religious authority. The imam forms part of a complex of power; he is not in a position of leadership. His authority stems from the fact that he directs the prayer and holds responsibility over the principal activities carried out in the mosque. The respect felt by followers toward the imam is a social factor: the imam is generally known, respected, and liked by the majority of members of the Turkish community.

What are the skills required to become an imam? This mainly depends on the *takva*, religious knowledge, and *kıraat* (*qirâ'ât* in Arabic). The *takva* is a form of religious virtue.[15] It is a notion which corresponds to the care to obey religious principles, to keep oneself free from sins, and to be

---

[11] This is the definition by Max Weber. See Weber, *Economie et Société* (Vol. 1), Paris, Pocket, 1995, p. 289.

[12] Ibid.

[13] This ritual is called *salât* in Arabic. In Turkish, the word *namaz* is used to talk about prayer, which is concerned mostly within the context of daily language. However, people use Arabic when reciting the Koran, calling to prayer, and praying.

[14] See Ignaz Goldziher who analyses the subject by citing the hadith of Buhkârî. Goldziher, *Le dogme et la loi de l'Islam*, Paris, Bookstore Geuthner, 1920, p. 253.

[15] The term *taqwâ* in Arabic is derived from the root word *wiqâya*, meaning protection.

pious. Religious knowledge is certified by diplomas. For Turks, most of the time, these diplomas are issued by the *imam hatib lisesi* and by a theological faculty in Turkey. The vast majority of Turkish imams in Belgium (except the Shiite imams) have graduated from these schools or universities. They have a conception of Islam in accordance with Sunnite, Hanafite, and *mâturîdîs* principles.[16] Lastly, the imam is required to be able to do the right *kıraat*; namely, the correct reading and correct method of reciting the Koran in Arabic.[17]

The imam thus constitutes a traditional and central authority figure in Sunnite and Shiite Islam. The imam's legitimacy should not be thought of independently of the Muslim tradition and his position in the religious field. However, among the Alevis, there is another central figure, namely the *pîr*, also called *dede* (the authentic and original term is *pîr*). The *pîr* is an actor who runs the ritual of *cem*. It should be noted that the *pîr* is not equivalent to the imam: they are two different figures, for different rituals, within different denominations. One can compare the *pîr* to the sheikh in Sunnite Islam, whose importance is about to diminish in the Muslim world. Providing the equivalent can help to better understand what represents the *pîr*, but could pose a risk of not grasping the specificity of this figure. For example, among the Alevi Erenler, these two authority figures (*dede* and imam) are present at the same time, meaning that they co-exist.

The nature of traditional power varies according to the means of mobilization and the type of religious movement. Among the Turkish or Kurdish Nurcu and Sufi, there are other authority figures who are historically formed. However, these figures should not be considered as a replacement or an equivalent to the imam, because the Nurcu and Sufi, like other Islamic group members, follow the imam when they pray in a mosque. The Nurcu groups are characterized to some extent by the leadership of the *abi* (male) and *abla* (female), whereas the Sufi groups are run by the sheikh. *Abi* literally means older brother, and *abla* older sister, in Turkish. Both are considered to be responsible for the Nurcu house to lead the *sohbet*, the reading; in other words, in the informal organization, they have

---

[16] Maturidism (Mâturîdiyya in Arabic) is a theological school which defends the principles of *ehl-i sünnet* (Sunna followers). Its name is derived from Imam Mâturîdî who lived in the tenth century.

[17] To be recognized as an imam by the Muslim Executive of Belgium, the imam is required to pass an oral exam of the *kıraat* (reading). The imam, nominated by the Belgian state, receives training which is proposed and organized by the Muslim Executive.

a higher rank. But neither the *abi* nor the *abla* is a unique figure leading the *sohbet* or the reading, because there is no strict religious hierarchy in Nurcu circles. When a hierarchy is formed, it would be deemed not only religious, because psychological and social foundations should be considered as well. The main determinants for becoming an *abi* or *abla* are the capacity to have assimilated the *Risale-i Nur*, the *takva*, availability, and altruistic action.

In addition, the sheikh is a figure of traditional authority. This term literally means old man in Arabic.[18] However, this text uses the term in a religious sense. Historically, the title of sheikh was mostly employed to refer to the advocates of *ehl-i sünnet*, apart from Shiism and mutazilism.[19] It was structured as a Sufi term—specifically, what guides the *mürid* (the disciples)—and shows the "right path" (*irşad*).[20] In Turkish, *er, ermiş*, and *erenler* are words akin to sheikh,[21] as reported in the Erenler association. In a Sufi *tarikat*, the title, which is transferred between generations, is based on a historical scheme of concatenation (*silsile*). It is necessary for a sheikh to possess qualities such as mastering the art of conservation of oral traditions, sharing the word (*sohbet adabı*), and having strong elocution, good relations with the *mürid*, a spiritual vision, and the capacity to experience the state of *vecd* (trance). Nowadays, this authority is absent in Belgium, except among the Sufis who are attached to a far-away sheikh (which will be examined in the following sections).

RELIGION AND BUREAUCRATIC, ADMINISTRATIVE, AND ASSOCIATIVE POWER

From the previous discussion, it is apparent that traditional authority figures are varied, and that the imam is assigned a more specific status as he plays a more important role in the mosque, which is a sacred place for Muslims. This section examines bureaucratic, administrative, and associative forms of power and their relationship with religion. Considering religious associations have more or less common traits regardless of their

---

[18] In Arabic and the Ottoman Turkish language, the plural of the term is *Şuyûh* and *Meşâyih*, in contemporary Turkish *Şeyhler*.

[19] Ahmet Yücel, "Şeyh", *Türkiye Diyanet Vakfı İslâm Ansiklopedisi*, Vol. 39, 2010, p. 50.

[20] Reşat Öngören, "Şeyh", *Türkiye Diyanet Vakfı İslâm Ansiklopedisi*, Vol. 39, 2010, pp. 50–52.

[21] Ibid., p. 50.

affiliations with Islamic movements, this section studying modern power does not differentiate between specific affiliations beyond a few significant characteristics. The researcher's use of generalized descriptions for associations should not be considered as an issue of specification, but rather as a necessary generalization, because some characteristics are universal to all associations.

A power is bureaucratic if it is exercised by a particular administrative office, and the propositions, decisions, dispositions, and regulations are established in writing.[22] The term "bureaucracy" has been used in European languages for some centuries, notably through the contribution made by Max Weber, and scholars usually apply it to the study of official organizational power. In Weberian sociology, the term is used to examine almost all sorts of rational, administrative, modern, complex power, regardless of whether it is in regard to the state or a private organization. What Bourdieu explains as "the objectification transmitted by the title and, more generally, all forms of official power [...], in the sense of written proof of qualification which provides legitimacy or authority,"[23] seems to generally match bureaucratic power. This occurs in these types of conditions because the legitimacy of power relations establishes itself between institutions, titles, positions, and jobs which are socially defined and formally guaranteed, instead of being established simply between individuals.[24]

As already noted, this concept of bureaucracy is used to describe the religious associations and federations in this study. This phenomenon concerns the power of the administrative branch of an association or federation whose sphere of action falls within the domain of civil, religious, and cultural society. It is relevant to comment on the context in which these structures emerged. Indeed, the legalization of religious movements partly explains the emergence of this bureaucracy, because they are compelled to adapt to the judicial system in which they officially operate and the resources offered to them.[25] But above all, it stems more from a necessity than a constraint imposed from the outside. The development of mosque

[22] Max Weber, *Economie et Société* (Vol. 1), p. 293.

[23] Pierre Bourdieu, "Les modes de domination," *Actes de la recherche en sciences sociales,* Vol. 2, No. 2, 1976, p. 125.

[24] Ibid., p. 125. While Bourdieu does not explicitly reference the term bureaucracy in his article, he defines one of its major characteristics—that of objectified relations, which extend to the domains of both national and international bureaucracy.

[25] As suggested above, power relations operate in a legal framework which influences the making of internal authority.

networks, associations, and relations (of which I have presented certain local historical examples and episodes in Houthalen and Verviers) resulted in the formation of administrative offices. If a network develops, it is almost inevitable that it will lead to an association (except when the political regime is too authoritarian or the action itself is completely anti-establishment). It is part of the process of changing in scale, in which the Diyanet, the BIF, the Union of Islamic Cultural Centers of Belgium, and other similar associations are included.

The essential characteristics of bureaucratic, administrative, and associative structures can be outlined as follows.

The first characteristic is the procedural and regulatory pillars on which these structures depend. Since the act is consistent with the outlined criteria, it is both rational and predictable.

Secondly, there is a division of labor. Religious organizations today include a social, cultural, and religious division of work. But why does such a division of work occur?

Emile Durkheim elaborated the notion of a division of labor in the industrial sector linked to the development of capitalism.[26] According to Durkheim, it is applicable to global society. However, I will apply this concept to the socio-cultural and religious fields. The mechanism of division results from the progressive differentiation of religious, social, and administrative activities, which in turn lead to the appearance of new tasks (an accounting department, namely *muhasebe* in Turkish), positions, figures, or authorities. Consequently, a bureaucratic organization develops wherein authority is shared between different roles and people. It is relevant to mention that in the aforementioned historical examples religious organizations developed in multiple ways, whether in Verviers, Houthalen, Brussels, or Antwerp. One can consider this division of power as a form of rationality and pragmatism. If the power is divided, authority is not held by a single person able to do everything. It is rational from a formal viewpoint.

When studying the structure of the Diyanet or BIF, or any similar mosque association, one notes different lines of authority for each department: for example, women's affairs, youth, and the board. The division of power operates according to competence, specialization, age, and gender. As authority is divided (the division here is not understood in a negative sense or segmentation), there is no longer a question of sole legitimacy.

---

[26] Émile Durkheim, *De la division du travail social*, Paris, PUF, 2007.

The roles and responsibilities are more or less shared voluntarily between actors.

A third characteristic is that power is relatively impersonal. This is why unique leadership is not applicable to associations. Neither the decision nor the collective act relies on just one person. There is a principle of collegiality which guides the associative group's action: the general assembly meets and decides unanimously. In addition to a general assembly, any nonprofit association is generally characterized by a board of trustees and a monitoring committee (though this can vary when it is a matter of a school or federation, etc.). The impersonal and collegial principle makes authority a more collective process (although power struggles at the individual level can emerge, like in almost all social, religious, and political groups). It is the federation or organization as a whole which holds authority, as is the case with the BIF or the Union of Islamic Cultural Centers in Belgium (UCCIB).

In spite of these features that one observes in classic bureaucracies, the bureaucracy of these associations and federations differs from classic bureaucracies. Bureaucracy formed according to social and religious fields does not necessarily function like a political field—for example, financial, ministerial, or bureaucracy. Comparatively, these bureaucracies are characterized by less conflict between superior and subordinates than modern bureaucracies, and hence differ from the characterization by Michel Crozier.[27] Crozier suggested that there exists a tension between the senior staff and subordinate employees in state bureaucracies, commercial enterprises, and even nonprofit organizations. In my field observations of religious associations and federations, I noted that the individuals, selected for their positions without discrimination, carry out their responsibilities in a subordinate manner which is both flexible and uncontested. The fact that there is less internal conflict in comparison with other types of classic or modern bureaucracies can be explained by the presence of a fraternal, non-materialistic spirit, as well as mutual interests like religious ideals.

Altruism is another characteristic that plays an important role in the emergence and persistence of these structures. Indeed, collective action is characterized by altruism, which in this case signifies voluntary work. As per the examples of Houthalen and Verviers, it is a socio-historical form of action. (It was immigrant workers who volunteered to build mosques and associations without compensation.) Altruism is a behavioral aspect among

[27] Michel Crozier, *Le phénomène bureaucratique*, Paris, Seuil, 1971.

high- and low-level positions, even though the concept is more difficult to apply to those in higher-level positions. A president of a federation or an association will gain social standing and will be financially recompensed for his or her work. Despite this reservation, I would suggest that altruism is present at various levels in associations and mosques, not only among the workers who build mosques and associations, but also among the imams and presidents of associations, those responsible for the youth and female branches, and those involved in the organization of activities.

Certain conclusions can be drawn about these significant facts which have so far been little explored in the social sciences. This process of rationalization and legalization leads to the emergence of new power holders. Thus, youths and women, who do not necessarily have authority within traditional power structures, gain power in associative and federative structures. They have certain types of competences and resources that enable their integration in cultural and religious systems; these sources can be altruistic action like volunteering, or symbolic and social capital like a knowledge of languages (French, Flemish, and Turkish), the ability to manage the group, and so on. In contrast to the traditional structures, which still exist, there are almost no heroes or leaders, but officials and volunteers within bureaucratic structures.

But can this type of structure exclude personal charismatic power? Absolutely not. However, as noted by Weber,[28] charisma is an unstable authority: once the charismatic person disappears, such a resource might disappear unless it has become a routine or is transferred to another person. The emergence of the charismatic man is irregular and does not constitute an absolute need. Associations or federations are undoubtedly mobilized by charismatic figures at times.[29] Yarbay in the Menzil group illustrates this point clearly.

Yarbay (Mehmet Ildırar) was born in Afyon in 1927. He received primary and secondary education there. His childhood and primary education occurred within the context of Kemalist reforms. He entered military school to pursue his studies initially at the high school level, and then in

---

[28] Max Weber, *Economie et Société* (Vol. I), pp. 326 and 330, and James S. Coleman, "Authority Systems", *Public Opinion Quarterly*, Vol. 44, No. 2, 1980, p. 158.

[29] This means that the role of charisma is reduced, but has not completely disappeared in bureaucratic and rational societies. See Edward Shils, *Center and Periphery: Essays in Macrosociology*, Chicago, University of Chicago Press, 1975. Lous Schneider, "Center and Periphery: Essays in Macrosociology by Edward Shils", *Journal for the Scientific Study of Religion*, Vol. 14, No. 4, 1975, pp. 417–418+420.

higher education. He served in the Turkish army for 27 years and retired in 1971 following the military coup. *Yarbay* means colonel. This military grade, which he previously had, was used as a nickname. The Menzil followers told me how he became a *mürid*. It was during a period of increased state repression against political and religious movements in Turkey. According to his disciples, Yarbay was sent to Menzil on a military mission aimed at tightening control over the brotherhood. He was so influenced by Sheikh Seyyid Abdülhakim El-Hüseyni (1902–1972) and the brotherhood that he left the army that same year and began participating in Sufi activities. He moved to Germany in 1983 following the military coup of 1980, which was far more repressive than the one in 1971. He died in 2012 and was buried in the village of Menzil in Adıyaman.

Yarbay's immigration to Dortmund is of paramount importance, as he played a charismatic role in the structuring of the brotherhood in Germany and Belgium. He held conferences (*sohbet*), particularly in Dortmund, but also from time to time in Belgium. Yarbay was so persuasive that most people who listened to him adhered to Sufism and joined the Menzil Brotherhood. I encountered many people who went to Dortmund every month and saw him in Belgium. His disciples referred to him so frequently that it would be inappropriate not to devote attention to his charismatic force in this study.

The issue of charisma could not be understood if these elements were not presented. Indeed, charisma is first and foremost a force embedded within this charismatic person's biography. His commitment to a brotherhood following a military career—at a time during which relations between the army and religious movements were problematic in Turkey—and life in Europe, where he built close contacts with the Muslims in Germany, Belgium, and the Netherlands, is quite exceptional. His biography contains charismatic elements. The continued use of the title Yarbay by his disciples can be interpreted as a charismatic element because of the opposition it represents between "being a former soldier" and "becoming a Sufi leader." Furthermore, the emergence of a charismatic personality is linked to a context of crisis. This crisis is twofold among Muslim immigrants. It is first an identity crisis and occurs following relocation to a new non-Muslim country. Secondly, it refers to the problems of a religious organization aimed at conserving and maintaining the Islamic faith. But what is the effect of charisma on the people I observed?

Yarbay was persuasive without being coercive. It is quite possible that his conversations with others progressively tapped into the souls of men

and women, leading them to become Sufi and pious. In this respect, charisma relates to the ability to be an orator, a preacher, enabling the transfer
of ideas and knowledge to disciples. But the spectacular effects of charisma
lie in its power to change things rapidly. This was primarily apparent in the
"prompt conversions" of the people who saw and listened to Yarbay.
Alternatively, this spectacular effect could be seen through the impact of
someone's first meeting with him—he often penetrated the mind and
imagination of people who saw and heard him for the first time.

Consequently, a combination of different types of power exists and can
be defined. Traditional power is not lone and isolated; rather, it is a branch
of a more complex web of authority. The case of the imam exemplifies this,
as he is a traditional authority figure who, at the same time, is part of the
power. Just as it is formal by its existence on paper, his authority is also
legitimized through its connection to the power of associations and federations. None of these power structures, which include other authority
figures previously examined such as *abi* and *abla*, exclude charismatic
power, which emerges in a more unstable manner.

Islam as a Permanent Movement

My conceptualization of power in regard to religious mobilization and
associations, whether it concerns traditional, charismatic, or bureaucratic
authority, depends on the structural specificity of permanent relations, as
explained in Norbert Elias' work.[30] Indeed, social and religious activities
generate a recursive structure based on permanent relations. But why do
these relations become permanent? How do these permanent relations
operate? This section aims at answering these questions.

The essential assumption is that power is generated by tradition and
bureaucracy, but in order to persist, it must rely on permanent movement.
This perpetual movement is regulated by relationships of proximity and
distance (and obeys a temporal order).

Questions of proximity and distance deal with space and time; there are
several Turkish and Muslim movements, communities, and associations
occupying different space-times. The exhaustive approach becomes all the
more difficult because of the multiplicity of movements. Despite the difficulty of elaborating and articulating a vast body of knowledge, the

---

[30] Norbert Elias, *Qu'est-ce que la sociologie?*, Paris, Editions de l'Aube, Coll. Pocket, 1991
[1970], p. 107.

researcher persisted with this approach in order to explore religious practices in all their complexities: the plurality of the actors, events, and actions.
Hence, it seems necessary to clarify certain characteristics of these complex
relations before proceeding with the analysis. There is no single pattern of
close or distant relations. Although there are certain common elements
which will be outlined in the following section, the effects of proximity
vary. For example, the proximity of a mosque to its followers is contingent
upon their practice of prayer in this mosque; the proximity of an association to its members is through a sense of belonging; while for a school
proximity is reflected through the choice of families to enroll their children in a particular institution. As such, proximity does not always manifest in the same way: it can be symbolic, trans-local, trans-regional,
trans-national, or bureaucratic. These relations should not be understood
in a univocal manner, but rather in a multifaceted one.

Proximity and Territoriality Among the Turks

Before being a social and cultural phenomenon that influences religious
movements, proximity is a territorial construct. Territoriality signifies the
space commonly inhabited by Turkish Muslims, be it a village, city district,
or region. We can thus consider this notion at both a local and a national
level. It is beyond the scope of this study to examine how this Muslim territoriality was historically constituted in Belgian neighborhoods, villages,
and cities; instead, the aim is to show that territoriality is one of the conditions for proximity.

It is pertinent to identify certain characteristics of these territories
inhabited by the Turks based on field observations, even before discussing
the relationship between territories and religious groups.

In Belgium, the Turks, like other Muslim communities, inhabit the
same physical space, namely a street or neighborhood in a village or city.
There is no "suburban" urban phenomenon as we see in the Paris area,
such as Clichy-sous-Bois, Drancy, or Seine-Saint-Denis. These areas are
territorial agglomerations inhabited by Muslim or African immigrants relatively isolated from central Paris socially, culturally, and economically.[31]
The territorial configuration of Belgian cities differs. The Turks (like

---

[31] There are some Parisian districts where one finds neighborhoods predominantly inhabited
by Muslim and African immigrants, similar to the situation in Brussels. This remains different
from the phenomenon of segregated suburb in the Paris area which barely exists in Belgium.

North African and Muslim African communities) are not necessarily on the periphery or margins of the city ("margin" is used in the geographic sense). On the contrary, in cities like Brussels, the Turks live in Schaerbeek and St. Josse, two very central neighborhoods, along with Molenbeek and Laeken, which are not remote neighborhoods. Admittedly, Belgium has several types of territoriality, urban and rural, which vary from Brussels, to Wallonia, and to Flanders. These cities have different processes of industrialization and geographic culture, but Brussels is no exception. This type of territoriality is the same in Antwerp, Verviers, Liège, Heusden-Zolder, Ghent, and so on. Just like the north or south of Antwerp, these are central neighborhoods for business, transportation, education, and cultural centers; these are neighborhoods which host activities. Unlike impoverished neighborhoods and villages like Marchienne-au-Pont, Flemish agglomerates populated with Turks and other Muslim populations—like Houthalen, Beringen, or Maasmachelen—are not characterized by poverty. These are places which seem prosperous. In these places, particularly in Limburg, relationships between Turks and non-Turks or non-Muslims are more frequent, whether through neighborhood relationships (vicinity), recurring visits to restaurants and shops, or participation in Turkish festivals, such as *kermesses.*

After defining this inhabited territorial space, useful when contextualizing the physical space occupied by the Turks, the focus will shift to the link between proximity and territoriality. The map presented in Chap. 2, indicating the geographic locations of associations and mosques, also shows the residential concentrations of the Turkish population. Based on this parallelism, it is reasonable to emphasize the interdependence between social and religious relationships and territorial factors. The work of sociologists at the Chicago School reminds us how territorial proximity influences social relationships.[32] But what exactly do proximity and contiguity allow? In fact, there is no geographic distance between religious organizations, authority figures, and the Turkish community: they are located in the same space, which facilitates contact without needing to instigate it. This kind of proximity generates immediate and spontaneous encounters.

What kind of effects does this territorial proximity produce? Territory, namely the place which one occupies or resides in, be it a street, a

---

[32] Marie-Pierre Lefeuvre, "Proximité spatiale et relations sociales," in Alain Bourdin, Marie-Pierre Lefeuvre, Annick Germain (eds.), *La proximité. Construction politique et expérience sociale,* Paris, L'Harmattan, 2006. pp. 89–100.

neighborhood, or a village (like the chaussée de Haecht, Schaerbeek, Meulenberg, Beringen-Mijn), provides a physical element to the community. These spaces of varying sizes characterize the community as well as the association by providing them with a location.[33]

Robert Zajonc acknowledged that proximity increases the probability of communication and contact.[34] In social psychology, this argument applies mostly to interpersonal relationships between two or more individuals. For instance, if two pupils who sit side by side become friends, their friendship as an outcome of proximity is a probability, but not a given. This is not necessarily a simple causal relationship between friendship and proximity, because they could also fervently hate each other. The probability of territorial proximity having favorable effects on social interactions in immigrant societies is high, since the individuals and groups already have a shared language, religion, culture, and home country. These social interactions take on various social and spatial forms.

For example, territorial proximity produces the neighborhood: to be a neighbor, one needs to reside in a place of proximity. Altay Manço defines the neighborhood among the Turks of Belgium as "a cause and consequence of the phenomenon of concentration," which contributes to the formation of "locally structured communities (associations, institutionalized representations) and culturally organized communities (shops, meeting places, and religious services)."[35] Among the Turkish populations, as I will discuss more precisely below, such territorial proximity increases social capital, for instance membership in a social, communal, and economic network. In the economic sense, it favors the local and ethnic market (food service industry, purchase of products and foods in grocery stores, and so on) and occasionally facilitates employment and housing, or leads to rentier solidarity and clientelism (recognizable in Schaerbeek among Turks, but also in Molenbeek among North Africans). It also allows for rapid communication, since the men and women know each other. Lastly, since the space is characterized by signs and symbols which are not necessarily religious, but mostly ethnic and linguistic (restaurants, stores, written

[33] On the relationship between society and place, see Simmel, p. 676.

[34] Robert B. Zajonc, "Attitudinal effects of mere exposure", *Journal of Personality and Social Psychology. Monograph Supplement*, Vol. 9, No. 2, 1968, pp. 1–27.

[35] Altay Manço, "L'organisation des familles turques en Belgique et la place des femmes," *Cahiers d'études sur la Méditerranée orientale et le monde Turco-Iranien* [Online], 21, 1996, released on 04 May 2006, accessed on 02 October 2016. URL: http://cemoti.revues. org/564, p. 3.

or spoken language), it contributes to the construction of individuals' identity.[36]

Proximity also sometimes creates trust, a notion which I referenced earlier without fully elaborating on the mechanisms which produce it. As suggested by Niklas Luhmann, "an unconditional trust exists in families and small societies which cannot be automatically transferred to complex societies based on a division of labor. In them, trust must be rebuilt with the help of special institutions."[37] On the subject of the Diyanet, Chap. 2 stressed the fact that it is a state institution, ensuring a certain credibility and trust, although limited by the diversity of movements in Turkish communities. Luhmann's hypothesis, if linked with the mechanism of proximity—which he does not mention—can explain how trust in the Diyanet or the BIF is maintained, despite the fact that these religious structures have become complex bureaucratic societies. Friendship networks, social circles, and religious or socio-cultural services rendered to the society illustrate this adaptation. They reconstruct solidarity and ties, and consequently moderate the opposition between *Gemeinschaft* and *Gesellschaft* or *Cemaat* and *Cemiyet*.[38]

Proximity and Social Relations

Proximity delineates different forms of social relations between religious entrepreneurs and the social base. First and foremost, it corresponds to the relationship that authority figures have with the community. As previously underlined, authority must to be handled as a relationship of reciprocity. The relation of the imam with the *cemaat*—the mosque attendants—is an example of this. The religious characteristics of an imam's role render him by definition close to the community. Apart from the religious dimension, the imam is a familiar figure within the society. He is, at least, well known and respected, and as such develops interpersonal

---

[36] Michel Bassand, "Quelques brèves remarques pour une approche interdisciplinaire de l'espace," *Espace géographique*, Vol. 9, No. 4, 1980, pp. 299–301. I emphasize the ethnic and linguistic signs, as the religious signs are much less visible in the physical space. However, what makes Islam visible is the human body which wears a veil, beard, or the traditional Muslim clothing. This is far more than the space which exhibits the halal sign. For instance, mosques are only slightly visible from the exterior in Belgium or in Europe.

[37] Niklas Luhmann, "Confiance et familiarité. Problèmes et alternatives," *art.cit.*, p. 17.

[38] The topic of the article by Niklas Luhmann is different from this theme. For his argument in greater detail, see p. 17.

relationships.[39] The religious aspect of his profession and his knowledge likely increases his social capital, particularly in terms of respect and amiability. His social capital also depends on personal traits. The more an imam has the capacity to manage social relations, the greater is his social capital. Similarly, the extent of his Islamic knowledge and his capacity as an orator impact his social status and power. While certain qualities vary according to an individual's capacities and characteristics, the imam has a number of professional skills.

Similar arguments apply to internal relationships within any religious group, although the figures and forms of proximity are variable. Relations of *abi* with *şâkird*[40] (a student of *Risâle-i Nur*) and *abla* with *şâkirdiye* (a female student of *Risâle-i Nur*) are important examples of proximity within Nurcu circles. These relationships are not the same as an imam's relationship with the local Muslim community, because the imam is a particular figure who exercises a function in the mosque. Nonetheless, the relations of *abi* with *şâkird* and *abla* with *şâkirdiye* remain a mechanism of proximity. The vocabulary concerning these relationships already refers to brotherhood: *abi* is older brother, *abla* is elder sister in Turkish. The term "older" implies respect in the Turkish and Muslim cultures, but every notion of brotherhood in Islam is also a notion of proximity. It is derived from the realm of parenthood, but its meaning is more social and religious. The elder brother and sister transmit the religious message and contents of *Risâle-i Nur* (an interpretation of the Koran), and read them with *şâkird* and *şâkirdiye* while remaining close to them. Thus, Islamic principles and meanings are diffused within the social circle.

There are different degrees and manners in which people can have close social ties. Conversation (*sohbet*) is one of the most frequently observed empirical forms of social proximity. As a form of speech, it is mostly informal and not necessarily religious. It is partly social, partly cultural, partly religious, and can take place between religious actors and the social base wherever people congregate to socialize. The *sohbet* is generally fluid; its boundaries are almost indeterminate, as its topic can include several issues at the same time. The conversation can take different forms, such as *mütâlaa* (*mutâla'a* in Arabic), *müzâkere*, or *münâzara*, depending on certain

---

[39] The topic here is limited to the relationship of the imam with worshippers. The imam does not exercise authority over people outside this category.

[40] The term *şâgird* in Farsi and *şagirt* in Kurdish refer to a student. In Turkish, the term is used within the Nurcu community to refer to students of *Risâle-i Nur*.

principles. When the conversation rests on a criticism of thought, it is referred to as *mütâlaa*. It is *müzâkere* when it is interactive, and *münâzara* if it takes the form of a debate. These are terms derived from Muslim culture (Arabic, Turkish, Farsi, etc.) that are employed in Turkish Muslim circles, but the *sohbet* is not required to take such a precise and defined form. The conversation, in its varying forms, constitutes a configuration of diffusion and internalization of Islamic knowledge. This phenomenon also can be interpreted in terms of micro-power constructs in society, as an imam, *şakird*, *mürid*, *derviş*, or *pîr* usually addresses people daily through their words, gestures, and acts. They employ the vocabulary of the Islamic lexicon such as *hamd* (glorification), *şükür* (gratitude), *rahmet* (divine favor), and *selam* (peace), and these religious expressions structure relationships as a means of communication and orientation. Not only is speech addressed orally, but various symbols and signs of a religious body, like the beard, scarf, *cübbe* (a kind of frock coat), and *ferace* (a coat with long sleeves that some Muslim Turkish women wear), are part of the interaction. As Tarde suggested long ago, the café, restaurant, street, and house are varying fabrications of power, as conversations in these places influence the evolution of public opinion.[41] Conversations are not necessarily organized; they depend on territorial proximity, primarily the neighborhood, which yields regular occasions for spontaneous discussions among residents.

Nevertheless, relations of proximity cannot be reduced exclusively to certain figures of authority, as proximity characterizes the relationship of most associations with their social base. Those whose actions I qualified above as altruistic and voluntary also engage with close relations within the community. Such proximity determines sociability, namely "the desire to meet and form groups" in the sense of Maurice Agulhon.[42] In this respect, the *kermesse* (village fair) is a relevant example: it is a popular social festival organized by various associations (which are almost all affiliated with movements like the Diyanet, the BIF, or the Shias). They organize these festivals each season, and in particular during the spring and summer. It targets all age groups as well as men and women. As such, I observed men,

---

[41] Gabriel Tarde, *L'opinion et la foule*, Paris, PUF, 1989, p. 122.

[42] The definition of sociability is Maurice Agulhon's, cited by Madeleine Villard in her review of Maurice Agulhon, *La sociabilité méridionale, Confréries et associations dans la vie collective en Provence orientale à la fin du XVIIIe siècle*, Publications des Annales de la Faculté des lettres, Aix-en-Provence, série Travaux et Mémoires, n° XXXVI) in *Bibliothèque de l'Ecole des chartes*, tome 124 (2), 1966, p. 595.

women, and children present at several *kermesses*. The women in particular play a considerable role in the organizational process, gathering families and preparing the sale of products such as garments and food. The *kermesse* is not a religious celebration; rather, it is a social event embedded within a cultural framework. Charles Tilly and Sidney Tarrow noted that "the repertoire of actions draws from individual identities, social ties, and organizational entities which constitute daily social life."[43] The *kermesse* does not originate from Turkish and Muslim culture, it is originally a Dutch feast. Despite this, Turkish women organize *kermesses* in Anatolia, and this cultural event is organized by Turkish communities in Belgium as well. Flemish Belgians sometimes participate in these Turkish *kermesse*. The feast is characterized by festivities, eating, and drinking (tea, coffee, ayran [a cold drink made of yoghurt and water], etc.) It is this festive environment that allows the organizers to interact with the participants.[44]

Having discussed certain figures, forms, and manners of proximity, it is now necessary to examine what social proximity leads to. Proximity contributes to the strengthening of social ties and bringing associations together with the community. It gives them a sense of personal sameness between those who organize and the participants. Proximity fosters frame alignment,[45] a mechanism facilitating and favoring personal engagement in an Islamic movement. The associations link their senses of the world with the community, or the community is aligned with the religious association. As such, for example, a person will affiliate him- or herself with the UCCIB in order to participate in its cultural and educational activities, with a Sufi movement to learn and practice *tasawwuf*, or with the Nurcu movement to read *Risale-i Nur*.

Such an interactive and historical process simultaneously diffuses religious meaning, reality, and consensus, as can be observed in the case of conversation, thereby increasing religious man and woman's capacity to act (*agency*). It promotes the Muslim faith and its obligations (prayer, pilgrimage, funerals, etc.), as well as social and cultural plausibility that legitimizes the power of associations and federations.

---

[43] Charles Tilly and Sidney Tarrow, *Politique(s) du conflit*, Paris, Presses de Sciences Po, p. 52.

[44] There is also an intercultural aspect of *kermesses*, as they are open to everyone and non-Muslim Belgian people participate in them as well.

[45] David A. Snow, E. Burke Rochford, Steven K. Worden, Robert D. Benford, "Frame Alignment Processes, Micromobilization, and Movement Participation", *American Sociological Review*, Vol. 51, No. 4, 1986, pp. 464–481.

One can also think about the link between proximity and the religious and social relations of a group from an ontological point of view. Indeed, a religious group, like every social, cultural, and political group (circle, community, tribe, party, nation), is *in part* a social artefact.[46] It only exists by means of collective symbolic and practical construction.[47] As Pierre Bourdieu suggested, "a social group is more likely to exist and endure so far as the actors who construct it are closely situated in the social space."[48] Places of sociability play a role in such group constructs. For example, the majority of Turkish associations have a café called a *lokal* (the meeting room). It is a place of meeting, eating, reading (Turkish) newspapers, books, and celebrating. The *lokal* differs from traditional Turkish cafés located in Turkish neighborhoods for several reasons. There is only halal food and drink consumption; the men do not play poker there; and it is not solely reserved for men. Inside there are two spaces, one is for men and the other for women and children. It is a building adjacent to the mosque which one can access in a few steps in order to pray, and then return to the *lokal* for tea or coffee. This is one of the social and spatial places of proximity which provides the mosque with a "sociality" function.

The Relationship to the Distance

The term "distance" refers to the relationship with the native country, namely Turkey, and to the Muslim world more broadly. National (in the sense of Turkish nationality and citizenship), political, ethnic (parenthood and family ties), cultural, linguistic, and religious links interact with each other, forming the relationship with the native country. For instance, I noted that the Turkish media play a key role in the diffusion of homeland culture and politics. This observation confirms the argument by Kaya and Kentel:[49] although the Turks in Europe have recently established new TV channels, radio stations, and newspapers, the homeland media still has an important role in sustaining Turkish traditions and discourses among them. Religion is not the only determining factor of this relationship, since Turkish immigrants in Belgium maintain strong ties with the Turkish

---

[46] This comparison does not mean that these social formations are identical.
[47] Pierre Bourdieu, *Raisons pratiques. Sur la théorie de l'action*, Paris, Seuil, 1994, p. 55.
[48] Bourdieu, *op.cit.*, p. 55.
[49] Ayhan Kaya and Ferhat Kentel, *Euro-Turks: A bridge or a breach between Turkey and the European Union?*, Brussels, CEPS Publications, 2005, p. 48.

state and nation. It is thus sometimes difficult to know the extent to which religion plays a defining role. Without disregarding the complexity of these relationships, this section handles the question from a religious point of view to understand how distance plays a role in religious power.

In the case of the Diyanet, the relationship with Turkey is a particular one, as the organization itself is affiliated with the Turkish government. As a result, this link is much more bureaucratic and organizational than other Islamic movements in Turkey. The tie between them is, in this respect, political and diplomatic. As explained earlier, imams of Diyanet-affiliated mosques (even the ones recognized by the Muslim Executive) are nominated by the Presidency of Religious Affairs in Turkey. Thus, one of the central religious figures both comes from Turkey and remains regulated by the Turkish government. Furthermore, a significant part of the higher bureaucracy of the Diyanet in Europe, including in Belgium, are public servants in the Turkish ministries, like the religious attaché of the foreign ministry. This, however, concerns only the higher strata of the Diyanet and does not apply to every level of power. Associations and mosques operating on the local level have their own independent bureaucracies. The bureaucracy at this level is made up of locals (including men, women, and young people) who manage the activities of the mosque. As is the case in almost every association, the general assembly, council of administration, and committee of control are composed of locals from the community. It can be consequently inferred that the first component of the power comes from the native country, whereas a second, more popular component is found in Belgium.

The relationship to the native country is quite different for other religious groups (especially for the Süleymanlı and Milli Görüş). Their bureaucracy is entirely formed in Belgium, by people who have lived most of their lives in the country. Comparatively, their relationships with Turkey are far more symbolic and imaginary. Indeed, one notices a strong attachment to ancient symbolic leadership, which varies across religious groups. The Milli Görüş keeps an attachment to its emblematic leader, Necmettin Erbakan, the Nurcu to Said-i Nursi, and the Süleymanlı to Süleyman Hilmi Tunahan. These historical links are still relevant because the symbolic produces real effects: remote leadership is not effective leadership, but it remains in the collective imaginary. It functions as a source of legitimacy: people read, speak, and use their religious, cultural, historical, and political heritages to adopt them as exemplary models.

These symbolic and imaginary ties are all the more distinctive in the Sufi movement, the Menzil. Indeed, this group has a living sheikh, whereas neither Said-i Nursi nor Erbakan, who are now both dead, were sheikhs. The followers of the Menzil Brotherhood are strongly attached to the sheikh Abdulbaki Erol Gavs-ı Sani, who lives in Adıyaman, a Kurdish province in the southeast of Turkey. This link is spiritual and involves characteristics common to Nakşi or Sufi groups across the Muslim world. Among themselves, followers of Menzil frequently recount the *menkıbes* (stories) on the life of the sheikh and his descendants. These are then used as a reference for their religious behavior and as a structure for their Sufi identity.

The Alevis and the Shia differ from other groups. A historical and genealogical relationship of authority exists in the Erenler. Indeed, the Alevi Erenler have a *dede* in Belgium, who comes from the family of Şahbaz. As previously described, they are strongly attached to the village of Karacalar and the religious community is managed by the Şahbaz family. They have been living in this village since the nineteenth century.[50] It was Hak Halili, a local historical figure, who settled there and taught the love of *ehl-i beyt*. The current Alevi *dede* is the grandson of Hak Halili, Bacım Sultan, and Kadir Ağa who, at the time, maintained the Alevi doctrine of *ehl-i beyt* in Karacalar. The tombs of these saints are in Karacalar, as well as an Alevi *tekke*. The saints are venerated and their tombs (*türbe*) are visited as places of pilgrimage (*ziyâret*).

Turkish-speaking Shiites have a conception of religious authority that does not exist among the Sunnis. The authoritative structure begins with the *Marja'iyya* institution, the title and function of which are assigned to jurisconsult scholars capable of interpreting religious precepts. This power stems from the doctrine of *imâmat* in duodecimal Shiism. The *müctehid* (mujtahid) is a representative of the vanished imam during his absence. The term *müctehid* is translated as "the one who interprets" and the title relates to the doctrine of *ithna 'ashari* or *isnaeşariyye*, according to the Shia conception of authority. The *müctehid* is a grand authority who exercises temporal and religious influence because he is the highest figure of the *marja-i taqlid*. The imitation, namely *taqlid*, does not concern *usûl-i din* (the basic principles of Islam), but consists of following the *müctehid*, a great scholar, apart from the basic principles. Today, there are two

---

[50] The *muhtar*, an elected local leader and equivalent to the mayor, is from the family of Şahbaz in Karacalar (Emirdağ).

influential actors among those who hold the status of *marja-i taqlid* in duodecimal Shiism: Ayatollah Khamanei in Iran and Sayyid Ali Husseini Sistani in Iraq. The fatwa of the *müctehid* is followed by the Shia community who recognize this authority. The followers then deal with religious questions and matters according to the particular interpretations issued by the recognized authority who has legitimacy to interpret religious questions. Shia followers act according to these interpretations, which are conceptualized as *amel*,[51] meaning acts carried out on the basis of religious precepts and principles.

Permanent Movement and Religious Temporality

Temporality here is understood as an integral part of a permanent religious movement that contributes to the persistence of the religious structure. Power and authority are not elements detached from Islamic practices. A religious movement cannot be reduced exclusively to sociocultural elements, because the religious community, which constitutes the social base of associations and movements, is created from religious rituals (*ibâdet*) organized according to the temporal order.

The study of rituals in relation to temporality matters for two reasons. First of all, religious rituals are carried out according to annual, monthly, weekly, and daily rhythms. As a reminder: prayer (*salât* in Arabic; *namaz* in Turkish), one of the five pillars of Islam, is practiced five times a day by worshippers. The imam leads the prayer when it is collectively performed in the mosque. Fasting (*sawm* or *oruç*), a period that changes annually according to the lunar calendar, is observed for one month every year. *Zekat* (*Zakat* in Arabic; alms or charity in English) is paid yearly to the poor or the needy by the sufficiently rich in accordance with Islamic norms. The pilgrimage to Mecca (*hac*: every Muslim's obligation at least once in their life if they have the necessary material means) also follows a temporal principle, as it is done during the lunar month of *dhû al-hijja*.

This temporality is more or less common to Muslims, even if Shia and Alevi communities differ in some respects. For example, Caferi Shiites pray three times a day and in addition to the month of Ramadan, they fast during the month of Muharram. Among the Alevis, the collective ritual of *cem* takes place primarily on Thursday evenings.

---

[51] This notion is not exclusively used by Shiites; Sunnis also employ it to talk about religious acts.

Secondly, there is a relationship between sacredness and time in Islam. Ramadan is a privileged month. The night of destiny (*Laylat al-Qadr* in Arabic, *Kadir gecesi* in Turkish) corresponds to one of the last ten days of the month of Ramadan (but is commonly celebrated on the twenty-seventh night of Ramadan). This night is particularly sacred, because in Muslim belief the Koran was revealed for the first time during that night. The Koranic text describes it as "the night greater than one thousand months" (in verse 3 of the Surah al-Qadr). Muslims go to the mosque more frequently during the month of Ramadan, in particular for the night prayer called *terâvih*. There is a three-day feast (*Ramazan Bayramı* in Turkish; *Eid al-Fitr* in Arabic) following the month of Ramadan.[52] Another sacred feast is the feast of sacrifice celebrated at the end of the period of pilgrimage.[53] Even if prayer is performed every day, Friday at noon is the collective prayer led by an imam after he delivers a sermon (called *hutbe* in Turkish; *khutba* in Arabic).

A few clarifications need to be made to avoid misinterpreting the argument of this section. The objective here is not just to study temporality in Islam. The text presents Islamic temporality because the religious is defined as a permanent movement of rituals that follow temporality. A large part of the permanent movement consists of religious routine. The relationship between religious rituals and temporality is stable. The rituals take place according to the temporal order, which contributes to the permanence of the religious routine. The practice of rituals is certainly not exclusively a question of power: it is faith which motivates and organizes them, as in all religions. Instead of arguing that religious men have a functionalist and utilitarian perspective, I suggest that religious power is not independent from this continuity and routine. The authority is closely linked with the organization of rituals, which are related to the basic principles of faith.

Alevism is a good illustration of how power depends on religious routine. The authority of the *pîr* (or *dede*) is weakened because the *cem* takes place less and less frequently, and because the relationship between the *pîr*

---

[52] In the lunar calendar, each month shifts by almost eleven days annually compared to the previous year. The month of Ramadan changes every year, because the months are not fixed as they are in the Gregorian calendar.

[53] According to the *fiqh* (jurisprudence) of the Hanafi school to which most Turks belong, the sacrifice of animals (like sheep, goats, or cows) is necessary (*vâcib* in Turkish; *wâjib* in Arabic), whereas in Malikism, Shafism, or Hanbalism (three other Sunni schools of Islamic law), it is Sunnah, namely linked with Islamic tradition, and it is encouraged.

and *tálib* is weakened or even broken. As this example deals with the discontinuity of a ritual and its outcomes, it demonstrates the importance of continuity. Nonetheless, when this example is compared with Sunni Islam's key ritual, some basic distinctions must be drawn due to structural differences. First of all, prayer is more frequent, as it is observed five times a day. Secondly, it is done more easily: to accomplish the prayer, there is no strict hierarchy which requires the presence of multiple figures, as in the ritual of *cem*. These examples are significant when trying to understand the extent to which the link between the permanence of authority and religious rituals is essential.

CHAPTER 4

Conclusion: Community (*Cemaat*) and Association (*Cemiyet*)

Abstract In order to preserve religious belief and identity, Muslim communities build associations. The local and trans-regional contexts influence these mobilizations, as Muslims are a minority living in an intercultural and interreligious environment in Europe. Within these communities and associations, the power structure is varied. Indeed, the religious field interacts with cultural, economic, and political fields, leading to a variety of resources, legitimacies, and figures of authority that mobilize societies in proximity and from a distance.

Keywords Religious authority • Legitimacy • Tradition • Charisma • Bureaucracy

The objective of this research was to present the principal Muslim movements among the Turks in Belgium and to study these movements from the angle of certain transversal themes. These movements arose from the mobilization of people who immigrated to Belgium from rural Anatolia in the 1960s and 1970s. In their common subjectivity, Muslim immigrants carried the risk of not being able to preserve their identity and belief due to the change of their milieu, as this new milieu was neither Muslim nor Turkish. This is when Muslims of Turkish origin begin to see "their lives

© The Author(s) 2020   89
M. Orhan, *Islam and Turks in Belgium*, New Directions in Islam,
https://doi.org/10.1007/978-3-030-34655-3_4

as a series of traps,"[1] leading to the necessity of forming groups, providing a community to preserve their identity. It is for this reason that circles of sociability appeared. This perspective corresponds to the problematics of minorities; Muslims constitute a minority community in Europe. It is not a passive minority, but rather an active minority in the sense of Serge Moscovici.[2] There are indeed possibilities of action and organization for this minority to become active thanks to mobilization.

The mobilization of Turkish Muslim immigrants is not based on radicalism, fundamentalism, or violence, terms regularly used by the media or many scholars to deal with the position of Muslims in contemporary Europe. The problem of radicalism is real and needs to be rigorously studied, but it cannot be regarded as a unique paradigm to deal with Islamic groups (neither in Belgium nor anywhere else in the world).[3] One cannot adopt the same approach to analyze Islamic movements without taking into account their particularities, vision of the world, and repertoires of action either. Studies on the Muslim groups operating in civil society should take into account the Turkish and Belgian intercultural contexts and interreligious contexts between Muslims and non-Muslims, which involve several forms of relations, including different tensions, open and hidden conflicts, exclusions, inclusions leading the actors to search for Islamic moral support, reference groups, and benchmarks.

Thus, several movements came into being among the Turks, which rested on the model of organizations that were already preexisting in the Muslim and Turkish world, such as the Diyanet, the Milli Görüş, the Süleymanlı, the Nurcu, the brotherhood of Nakşibendi, the Alevis, and the Shia. The spheres of activities of these groups are similar, whereas their resources of mobilization are not completely identical. As previously presented, the impact, size, and frequency of their activities are variable. Ultimately, what descriptive and analytical conclusions congruent to all groups can be drawn? In spite of the diversity of these movements and their different internal and external structures of authority, one can proceed to certain common conclusions on these religious organizations.

---

[1] C. Wright Mills, *The sociological imagination*, London, Oxford University Press, 1959, p. 3.

[2] Serge Moscovici, *Psychologie des minorités actives*, Paris, Presses universitaires de France, 1991 [1979].

[3] The study by John O'Brien draws a similar conclusion on the Muslim youth in the USA. See O'Brien, *Keeping It Halal: The Everyday Lives of Muslim American Teenage Boys*, *op.cit.*

First of all, it is collective religious and socio-cultural action that organizes religious power under different types of authority. The field of religious power is so vast that there is not a unique authority which dominates and controls all aspects of religious life. An authority can emerge where there are mobilizations, problems, and collective demands. Likewise, it is possible that new mobilizations and initiatives lead to new lines of authority. For example, halal markets can develop an authority which certifies halal products according to Islamic criteria. The tuna market, an enterprise initiated by the Süleymanlı for distributing halal food, is an illustration. This is an example situated between the economic and religious fields.

Secondly, in the religious field, the structure of power appears as a way of adapting to the system. The actors adapt their religious and socio-cultural finalities to the context. These systemic integrations take place within the legal framework that authorizes and restricts the power of action. While this aspect concerns relations between the state and Muslim actors, relations between Islamic actors and Muslim societies also play a key role in this process. Thus, authority is to be thought of in terms of reciprocity, because it is not exercised on itself. It is exercised by many figures who have roles, competences, and material and symbolic resources that rest on the social base.

I have studied different configurations of power from such a perspective. For example, on the basis of his practices, an imam structures himself as a role, figure, and authority within the framework of a legal system, enabling him to hold a status under the condition that he possesses certain resources. These resources are determined according to Islamic criteria. They are actualized through interactions with the community or social base, and adapted to the administrative system of the country where he exercises this function.

Third, authority is not coercive. Rather, it is internalized and accepted as legitimate. Legitimacy rests on traditional, charismatic, and bureaucratic types of authority. The internalization and acceptance of these authorities address the psychological aspect that can explain how these legitimacies function at the individual level. Religious authority operates in a particular way because the individual, who obeys, feels sublimated; namely, those who succumb to these pressures feel the desire to participate in something which surmounts and transcends them. Furthermore, the social pact that links men and women with their equals lies in the act of belief and brotherhood required by religion. Such characteristics are not necessarily found in all forms of domination.

Finally and very importantly, the common point of these religious movements is that they express themselves as communities and associations. Collective action results in the community (*cemaat*) and the association (*cemiyet*), which constitute a specific field determined by different legal, social, cultural, and psychological regimes. The passage from the community to the association is not a change, but an adaptation to the system. In modern Muslim societies, communities and associations are interdependent. The communities establish the associations which represent them and manage their affairs. These organizations depend on the combination of mechanical and organic, vertical and horizontal, near and far-away solidarities.

BIBLIOGRAPHY

Abadan-Unat Nermin, *Turks in Europe. From Guest Worker to Transnational Citizen*. New York and Oxford, Berghahn Books, 2011.

Agulhon Maurice, *Le cercle dans la France bourgeoisie: 1810–1848. Etude d'une mutation de sociabilité*, Paris, Armand Collin, 1977.

Ahmad Feroz, *The Making of Modern Turkey*, London & New York, Routledge, 2003.

Akgün Ali, "Tasavvuf insanlığa ne vaat ediyor?", *Semerkand*, No. 157, 2012, pp. 32–39.

Allievi Stefano, *Les convertis à l'islam: les nouveaux musulmans d'Europe*, Paris, L'Harmattan, 1999.

Allievi Stefano, *Conflicts over Mosques in Europe: Policy Issues and Trends*, London, Alliance Publishing Trust, 2009.

[Anonymous] *IGMG Tanıtım Katoloğu*, Cologne, IGMG – Islamische Gemeinschaft Millî Görüş, 2014.

Balta Paul, *Islam, Civilisation et Sociétés*, Paris, Editions de Rocher, 1991.

Bassand Michel, "Quelques brèves remarques pour une approche interdisciplinaire de l'espace", *Espace géographique*, Vol. 9, No. 4, 1980, pp. 299–301.

Bayat Şirali, *Caferi Mezhebinde Namaz ve Oruç*, Istanbul, Sekaleyn yayınevi, 1996.

Berkes Niyazi, *The Development of Secularism in Turkey*, Montreal, McGill-Queen's University Press, 1964.

Bourdieu Pierre, *Esquisse d'une théorie de la pratique; précédé de Trois études d'ethnologie kabyle*, Genève, Droz, 1972.

Bourdieu Pierre, "Les modes de domination", *Actes de la recherche en sciences sociales*, Vol. 2, No. 2, 1976, pp. 122–132.

Bourdieu Pierre, *Raisons pratiques*, Paris, Seuil, 1994.

© The Author(s) 2020   93
M. Orhan, *Islam and Turks in Belgium*, New Directions in Islam,
https://doi.org/10.1007/978-3-030-34655-3

Bursalı Necati M., *Mezhebler Tarihi*, Istanbul, Ailem, Unknown date.

Coleman James S., "Authority Systems", *Public Opinion Quarterly*, Vol. 44, No. 2, 1980, pp. 143–163.

Coleman James S., "Authority, power, leadership. Sociological understandings", *New Theology Review*, Vol. 10, No. 3, 1997, pp. 31–44.

Crozier Michel, *Le phénomène bureaucratique*, Paris, Seuil, 1971.

Damar Hasan, *Avrupa'da Milli Görüş Hareketi* (2 Vol.), Istanbul, Gonca Yayınevi, 2013.

Dassetto Felice, *L'iris et le croissant*, Louvain-la-Neuve, Presses universitaires de Louvain, 2011.

Desama Claude, "L'age d'or de Verviers", *Conférence le 7 janvier 2013 à l'université de Liège* (Accessed in 10/02/2017 on https://www.ulg.ac.be/upload/docs/application/pdf/2013 02/59_lage_dor_de_verviers__2_.pdf).

De Tapia Stéphane, Dumont Paul, Jund Alain (eds.), *Enjeux de l'immigration Turque en Europe*, Paris, L'Harmattan, 1995.

Dufoix Stéphane, "Nommer l'autre", *Socio*, 2016 (7), pp. 163–186.

Durkheim Emile, *De la division du travail social*, Paris, PUF, 2007.

Elias Norbert, *Qu'est-ce que la sociologie?*, Paris, Editions de l'Aube, Coll. Pocket, 1991.

Elias Norbert, *Engagement et distanciation*, Paris, Fayard, 1993.

Erbakan Necmettin, *Davam*, Ankara, MGV Yayınları, 2014.

Giddens Anthony, *Central problems in social theory: action, structure and contradiction in social analysis*, London, Macmillan, 1979.

Goldziher Ignaz, *Le dogme et la loi de l'Islam*, Paris, Librairie Geuthner, 1920.

Halbwachs Maurice, *La mémoire collective*, Paris, PUF, 1950.

Haşimî S. Muhammed Saki, *Arifler Yolunun Edepleri*, Istanbul, Semerkand, 2014.

Ibn al-ʿArabî, *al-Futûhât al-Makkiyya* (9 Vol.), Bayrût, Dâr al-Kutub al-ʿIlmiyyat, 1999.

Ildırar Mehmet and Çağıl Ahmet, *Mürşid-i Kâmil Kimdir?*, Istanbul, Şadırvan, 2012.

İmam-ı Rabbânî Ahmed Farukî Serhendî, *Mektûbat-ı Rabbânî* (3 Vol.), Istanbul, Akit, 1998.

İslam Toplumu Milli Görüş, *IGMG Temel Eğitim Müfredatı*, Kerpen, IGMG e.V., 2010.

İslam Toplumu Milli Görüş, *Avrupa 4. Eğitim Şurası*, Kerpen, 2010.

Jenkins Richard, *Pierre Bourdieu*, London, Routledge, 1992.

Kaimi Asgar Üstat, *40 Derste Ehl-i Beyt İnançları*, Istanbul, Kevser yayın, 2007.

Kaya Ayhan, *Islam, Migration and Integration: The Age of Securitization*, London, Palgrave Macmillan, 2009.

Kaya Ayhan and Kentel Ferhat, *Euro-Turks: A bridge or a breach between Turkey and the European Union?* Brussels, CEPS Publications, 2005.

Kaya Ayhan and Kentel Ferhat, *Belgian-Turks: A bridge or a breach between Turkey and the European Union? Qualitative and quantitative research to improve understanding of the Turkish communities in Belgium*, Brussels, King Baudouin Foundation, 2008.

Khoojinian Mazyar, *Les Turcs à la mine. L'immigration turque dans l'industrie charbonnière belge (1956–1970)*, Louvain-la-Neuve, Editions EME, 2018.

Lebrecht Michaël, *Alévis en Belgique. Approche générale et étude de cas*, Brussels, Academia-Bruylant, 1997.

Lefeuvre Marie-Pierre, "Proximité spatiale et relations sociales", in Alain Bourdin, Marie-Pierre Lefeuvre, Annick Germain (eds.), *La proximité. Construction politique et expérience sociale*, Paris, L'Harmattan, 2006, pp. 89–100.

Lewin Kurt, *Resolving social conflicts. Selected papers on groups dynamics*, Gertrude W. Lewin (ed.). New York, Harper & Row, 1948.

Luhmann Niklas, "Confiance et familiarité. Problèmes et alternatives", *Réseaux*, No. 108, 2001, pp. 15–35. For English version, see "Familiarity, confidences trust: problems and alternatives", in Diego Gambetta (ed.), *Trust, Making and Breaking cooperative relations*, Oxford, Basil Blackwell, 1988, pp. 94–107.

Macionis John J., "The search for community in modern society: An interpretation", *Qualitative Sociology*, Vol. 1, Issue 2, 1978, pp. 130–143.

Manço Altay, "L'organisation des familles turques en Belgique et la place des femmes", *Cahiers d'études sur la Méditerranée orientale et le monde Turco-Iranien* [Online], 21, 1996, online publication on 04 May 2006, accessed on 02 October 2016. URL: http://cemoti.revues.org/564.

Manço Altay and Manço Ural (eds.), *Les Turcs de Belgique*, Brussels, Info Türk and CESRIM, 1992.

Manço Ural, "Identifications religieuses et jeunes issus de l'immigration: une recherche menée avec les travailleurs sociaux de Schaerbeek (Bruxelles)", *Forum*, No. 128, 2010, pp. 39–48.

Manço Ural, "Accueil et institutionnalisation de l'islam au niveau municipal: le cas de la communauté turque de Schaerbeek", in J. Gatugu, S. Amoranitis A. Manço (ed.), *Reconnaissance de l'islam dans les communes d'Europe. Actions contre les discriminations religieuses*, Paris, L'Harmattan, 2005, pp. 83–102.

Manço Ural and Kanmaz Meryem, "From Conflict to Co-operation Between Muslims and Local Authorities in a Brussels Borough: Schaerbeek", *Journal of Ethnic and Migration Studies*, Vol. 31, No. 6, 2005, pp. 1105–1123.

Mardin Şerif, *Religion and Social Change in Modern Turkey. The case of Bediüzzaman Said Nursi*, Albany, State University of New York Press, 1989.

Mills C. Wright, *The sociological imagination*, London, Oxford University Press, 1959.

Moscovici Serge, *Psychologie des minorités actives*, Paris, Presses universitaires de France, 1991 [1979].

O'Brien John, *Keeping It Halal: The Everyday Lives of Muslim American Teenage Boys*, New Jersey, Princeton University Press, 2017.

Öngören Reşat, "Şeyh", *Türkiye Diyanet Vakfı İslâm Ansiklopedisi*, Vol. 39, 2010, pp. 50–52.

Rigoni Isabelle, *Mobilisations et enjeux des migrations de Turquie en Europe de l'Ouest*, Paris, L'Harmattan, 2001.

[Saadet Partisi], *Saadetin Temel Esasları*, Unknown place and date.

Sägesser Caroline and Torrekens Corinne, "La représentation de l'islam", *Courrier hebdomadaire du CRISP*, n° 1996–1997, 2008/11, pp. 5–55.

Said-i Nursi, *Tarihçe-i Hayat*, Istanbul, Envar Neşriyat, 1995.

Sartre Jean Paul, *Critique de la raison dialectique* (Two volumes), Paris, Gallimard, 1960.

Schiffauer Werner, "Migration and Religiousness" in T. Gerholm and Y.G. Lithman (eds.), *The New Islamic Presence in Western Europe*, London and New York, Mansell, 1988, pp. 146–158.

Schneider Lous, "Center and Periphery: Essays in Macrosociology by Edward Shils", *Journal for the Scientific Study of Religion*, Vol. 14, No. 4, 1975, pp. 417–418+420.

Selâhaddin İbn-i Mübârek El-Buhârî, *Enîsü't Tâlibîn ve Uddetü's Sâlikîn Makâmât-ı Nakşibendiyye*, Istanbul, Buhara, 2010.

Shils Edward, *Center and Periphery: Essays in Macrosociology*, Chicago, University of Chicago Press, 1975.

Simmel Georg, *Sociologie. Etudes sur les formes de la socialisation*, Paris, PUF, 1999.

Snow David A., Rochford E. Burke, Worden Steven K., Benford Robert D., "Frame Alignment Processes, Micromobilization, and Movement Participation", *American Sociological Review*, Vol. 51, No. 4, 1986, pp. 464–481.

Sunier Thijl and Landman Nico, *Transnational Turkish Islam: shifting geographies of religious activism and community building in Turkey and Europe*, Basingstoke, Palgrave Macmillan, 2015.

Tabatabâi Allame, *Tüm boyutlarıyla İslam'da Şia*, Istanbul, Kevser Yayın, 2009.

Tarde Gabriel, *L'opinion et la foule*, Paris, PUF, 1989.

Tilly Charles, *From Mobilization to Revolution*, Reading, MA: Addison-Wesley, 1978.

Tilly Charles and Tarrow Sidney, *Politique(s) du conflit*, Paris, Presses de Sciences Po, 2008.

Torrekens Corinne and Adam Ilke, "Belgo-Marocains, Belgo-Turcs – (auto)portrait de nos concitoyens", Brussels, Fondation Roi Baudouin, 2015. Availabe at: www.kbs-frb.be/fr/

Tönnies Ferdinand, *Communauté et société: catégories fondamentales de la sociologie pure*, Paris, PUF, 2010 [1922].

Tunahan Süleyman H., *Kur'ân Harf ve Harekeleri*, Istanbul, Fazilet Neşriyat ve Ticaret, 2012.

Uysal Ali, "Menkıbeler ne söyler", *Semerkand*, No. 157, 2012, pp. 20–24.

Villard Madeleine, "Maurice Agulhon. La sociabilité méridionale, Confréries et associations dans la vie collective en Provence orientale à la fin du XVIIIe siècle", (Publications des Annales de la Faculté des lettres, Aix-en-Provence, série Travaux et Mémoires, n° XXXVI, 1966) in *Bibliothèque de l'Ecole des chartes*, 1966, tome 124 (2), pp. 595–596.

Weber Max, *Le savant et le politique*, Paris, Union générale d'éditions, 1963.

Weber Max, *Economie et Société*, Paris, Pocket, 1995 [1971].

Yavuz M. Hakan, *Islamic Political Identity in Turkey*, Oxford, Oxford University Press, 2003.

Yeşil Camii Houthalen, *40 yıl Yeşil Camii*, Houthalen-Helchteren, Unknown Date.

Yıldırım Abdullah, "Hac Müslümanların ülfet duygusunu kazanmasına vesile olur", *Camia*, 7 July 2017, pp. 6–7.

Yücel Ahmet, "Şeyh", *Türkiye Diyanet Vakfı İslâm Ansiklopedisi*, Vol. 39, 2010, pp. 50.

Zajonc Robert B., "Attitudinal effects of mere exposure", *Journal of Personality and Social Psychology. Monograph Supplement*, Vol. 9, No. 2, 1968, pp. 1–27.

Index[1]

---

[1] Note: Page numbers followed by 'n' refer to notes.

Printed in the United States
By Bookmasters